Oh How Can I
Keep on Singing?

OH HOW CAN I KEEP ON SINGING?

Voices of Pioneer Women

Poems by JANA HARRIS

Ontario Review Press/Princeton

Some of these poems have previously appeared,
sometimes in a slightly different form,
in the following journals:
"Committing the Landscape to Memory" and "Fever" in *Calyx*;
"Monday" and "Tuesday" in *Jeopardy*;
"Avalanche," "Check-a-ma-poo,"
and "This New Life" in *Ontario Review*; .
"Dutch Jake's Hell-Time Calendar," "Salmon City
Flood," "The Laundress by the Lake," and "My Brothers
Worked the Ranch, I Got the Mail Route" in *Overthewall*.

Library of Congress Cataloging-in-Publication Data

Harris, Jana.
Oh how can I keep on singing? : voices of
pioneer women : poems / by Jana Harris
1. Frontier and pioneer life—Washington (State)—Fiction.
2. Women pioneers—Washington (State)—Fiction.
3. Washington (State)—History—Poetry. I. Title.
PS3558.A646203 1993 811'.54—dc20 93-15970
ISBN 0-86538-079-1 (pbk.)

Typesetting by Backes Graphic Productions
Printed by Princeton University Press

ONTARIO REVIEW PRESS
Distributed by George Braziller, Inc.
60 Madison Ave., New York, NY 10010

for Kathy, my Haight-Ashbury roommate

I would like to thank K. E. Ellingson, who read and commented on each draft of each poem countless times; Mark Bothwell, Raymond Smith, Maxine Kumin, Alicia Ostriker, Lorna Mack, Cindy Derway, and Leigh Bienen for their insight, help, and encouragement; Robin Straus for her perseverence; Joyce Carol Oates for her inspiration and help; and Lisa McKhann for her map work and proofreading. I would also like to thank Gene Fitzgerald for giving me access to privately published information on her grandmother, Lucinda Davis, and other Okanogan pioneers; and to Bill Kohls and the Okanogan County Historical Society for their help and assistance. Also I would like to thank Louise Reeve and Emil B. Fries for their reminiscences of the life of their mother, Anna Fries; and Joan Maiers for letting me read fragments of the homesteading notes made by her grandmother, Catherine Heaton. Finally, I am indebted to the Washington State Arts Commission for their support of this project.

CONTENTS

PHOTOGRAPHS

N

CANADA
Washington

CANADA
Washington

Similkameen River

Lake Osoyoos

Nighthawk
Oroville
Chesaw
Hee Hee Stone

Chiliwist

Mountains

Loomis
(Ragtown)

Omak Mission

Colville Reservation

Tonasket

Cascade

Mountains

Mazama

Mineral Hill

Conconully

Aeneas

Spokane

Winthrop

Ruby
Salmon Creek
Okanogan River

Riverside

Methow River

Buzzard Lake

Loup Loup Creek
Spring Coulee

Omak

Twisp River

Silver

Omak Creek

Okanogan
Alma

Malott

Methow

Sawtooth
Mountains

Brewster Flat
Virginia City

Old Fort Okanogan

Wild Goose Bill Condon Ferry

Nespelem
Indian Agency

Lake Chelan

Pateros

Columbia River

Grand Coulee Dam

Columbia River

Entiat

Mountains

Cut Wood

The Grand Coulee

Columbia River

Waterville

Coulee City

Icicle

Wenatchee River

Wenatchee

Seattle

Ellensburg

The
Okanogan

5 miles

Oh How Can I
Keep on Singing?

CATTLE-KILLING WINTER, 1889–90

We walked, of course.
Omaha to Walla Walla: 5 months, 3 days.
My husband, Nathan Sloan (known as Kentucky),
a fireman on the Missouri-Louisville line,
worked years tallowing valves
before the railroads fell on slack times.
He lost his job and the farm.

In Walla Walla, rested our oxen before
the baby—christened Caleb—was born,
walked another week north to where
Loop Loop Creek crosses the Okanogan.

Long days, high clouds, temperatures in the 90's.

Made a land claim, went to Buzzard Lake
to wash and water our stock,
met a miner, Dutch Jake, and his dog,
who infected my husband with gold fever.
Came back, found our claim jumped,
went up creek, made another. The only law
against selling black powder to an Indian.

Milled lumber too costly—not even a board
for a coffin. So cut and hewed logs for a cabin,
our lead ox hauling through mire.
Local talk had it winters too mild
to necessitate a barn.

Humidity high. Nighttime temperatures falling.

Mosquitoes so thick, Nathan had to stand
above me as I cooked, battling them off
with a towel. Morning coffee required
constant skimming, while bugs
in our mash appeared as caraway.

Deer were so plentiful they staggered
for lack of forage and could be had by clubbing.
November 1, ten venison hams hung from our eaves.

Nights getting longer, though unseasonably warm.

Just before New Year's, I awoke to ice
in the washbasin. Snowed nineteen inches.
Temperatures dropped. Snow crusted hard enough
to cut the lead ox's tendon.
John Other Day, Cut Nose, and their squaws
came daily to our door demanding flour.
Oats: six cents a pound; potatoes, five;
hay, a hundred a ton if you could find it.

Forty below by mid-month. The sun never shone.

Our oxen froze in the fields,
the twin calves dead at the milch cow's side,
the last of our hay in front of her.
Five feet of snow and blizzarding winds
for thirteen consecutive days.

The only drinking water, melted snow;
the only wood, our furniture.
Nathan sawed frozen meat from the dead,
feeding it to what stock remained.
I soaked rags in the blood of offal, giving
the baby suck. God Be Praised, he thrived.

Up on Buzzard Mountain, prospectors
were trapped in their mines—the artillery
of avalanche thundered through our valley.
When he tried to leave, Dutch, his mule and hound,
were buried—the dog dug its way out.
Ours was the first cabin he came to.

Brought the two living cows and one horse
into our lean-to kitchen, supped with us
on flour mash and seed potato.
If we went anywhere, it was hand-over-hand

4

over ice. No mail for weeks,
river frozen, the railroad snowbound.
A stranger who went through on snowshoes,
said a neighbor's wife died of laudanum
taken with suicidal intent.
Flour and sugar gone, rumor our daily bread.

When the ice melted, the creeks swelled
bringing typhoid which weakened my husband.
After pneumonia, he looked worse
than any at Andersonville and was unable
to help with chores.

First day of March. Days longer. Heavy fog.

The stock were enfeebled by hunger.
Balding from rain scald, hair fell in sheets
from their hides. When the spring grass
came on, they were too weak to graze,
collapsing like long-legged insects.
Ill myself, I crawled out to help, Caleb on my back:
right hoof forward, left knee bent, sometimes
it took a rail under the rump to raise them.

Most ranchers went under.
Some took twenty years to repay loans
on herds that perished, and then
only when they sold off their farms.
But the two cows left to us begat others
who begat the thousand head
Caleb and his sons graze in this valley.

I was born Effie Rebecca, named for my mother,
but forever after that cattle-killing winter,
my husband called me by another.
Years ago he went to the stone orchard,
my place beside him ready: "SLOAN, Nathan
known as Kentucky, and Wife, Born Again '89
as God's handmaiden, Faith."

Long Days. High clouds. Temperatures in the 90's.

AVALANCHE

Mary Brisky,
Rattlesnake Canyon, February 1888

i.
I remember it this way:
That morning we sat down to breakfast,
me, mama, and the traveling Reverend.
My baby sister was on the floor
next to the sewing machine.
On the table, three blue bowls
filled with oatmeal.
It had a smoky taste that I'll never forget.
Sepin was outside shoveling snow
off the roof. My father was up on the bluff
cutting trees, snaking them down the mountain.
When a tree fell, there was the noise
of lightning lash and as it hit the ground,
thunder shook our cabin—those trees
were twenty feet around, some of them.
When baby crawled under the table,
I was afraid she'd burn herself
on the hot stones mama had
put there to warm our feet,
so I stooped to pick her up.

ii.
"What is your only comfort in life and death?"
Reverend Beggs's voice was far away.

I was lying on top of baby
who was screaming. I didn't
realize what was smothering me,
until her breath melted the snow.
Mama was nearby. I could hear,
but couldn't see or touch her.
She spoke calmly to us:
"Lie quietly and breathe as lightly as possible."

The baby kept screaming 'til I thought
my head would split.
"Are you hurt?" mama asked,
"Can you wiggle your arms and legs?"
I could. The baby was thrashing beneath me,
beating with her fists.

The Reverend's voice was shallow.
"From whence do you know your sin and misery?"
No one answered. Mama said to me:
"Mary, the first thing to know about a baby
is to keep her warm and dry."
The baby howled louder. Everything around us
was wet and cold.
"Don't let her little butt get red," mama said.
"For croup, rub her chest
in rendered mutton and turpentine."

The Reverend asked, "How are you delivered?"
Mama said, "Mary, you can get sixty loaves
of bread from a sack of flour,
if you're frugal. I always could."
I said, yes, and then she said, "Remember
to seal your crock of sourdough
with a layer of water, seal your buttermilk
the same way." I reminded her
it was my job to milk the cow and hers to churn.
She said now I would have to both milk
and churn. "Roasted barley is the best
substitute for coffee," she said.
"Use the juice of boiled corn cobs
for sweetener, and don't drink it up
faster than you make it."

"Jesus did not die for everyone
as some believe," Reverend Beggs droned.
"If God chooses to elect you,
you cannot fight it."
"I want father," I said. Mama said I'd see him,

but she wasn't sure when.
"And your brother, too," she added.

Though I shivered, I felt sleepy.
The baby screamed herself out.
She was soaking, my body kept her warm.
"Mary," mother said, startling me awake.
"If Pokamiakin comes to the door with a knife,
hide the baby in the bread box." By now
Reverend's voice was barely a whisper.
This time when he asked, What is your only
comfort in life and death? Mama answered,
"That I am not my own.
That I belong to Jesus Christ."

"And from whence do you know your sin
and misery?" "From the word of God,"
mother and I said, our voices one.

"And how are you delivered?"
I waited for mama to answer, but she did not.

iii
We sat down to oatmeal at 8:30 that morning.
At 5:00, they pulled us out.
The wall of falling snow knocked
my brother out of the way.
It was the baby's screaming that told father
and Sepin where to dig.
The Reverend Beggs was dead.
Mama was dead.
The cow could not be saved.
High up on the opposite canyon wall
were splintered logs, bits of furniture,
the wheel of the sewing machine, and one
blue bowl amid shards of all the others.

The smoky taste of oatmeal
was still inside my mouth.

CHECK-A-MA-POO
(Steelshot Woman)

Colville Reservation, 1897 .

First the clothmen came
to the Valley at the Top of the World.
They wore hard shoes,
their legs like tree limbs,
their feet leaving strange prints in the snow.
They came downriver from
where the sun never goes, they came
thick as grasshoppers.

Eena, eena, eena they sang.
We pointed the way to the beaverwood.
Fox, muskrat, even the stink tail
they re-named "money fur."

A starving clothman once came
to my father's house
more than 50 snows ago.
We gave him dried groundhog.
The blanket across his back
was peeling away in strips.
We gave him a cape,
the silky inner bark of cedar.
He gave my father water
the color of peat, cold to the finger,
hot to the tongue.
When the clothman died
we buried him without his steelshot.

The next snow
the first blackrobes appeared, singing,
"Whiskey, whiskey, throw it away."
They howled, "If you do wrong,
the devil will get you," in the manner of
a *talapus* talking to the moon.
It was a bad winter: hard rain,

11

deep snow; the blackrobes grew
bolder than coyotes.
A blackrobe came to our sweat lodge
and said, "Jesus died instead of you."
My father asked, "What is this to me?"
Chief Joseph who was also there said,
"My horse is faster than your horse."
The blackrobe went on and on:
God, his book; God, his talk; God,
his Jesus Christ Bostonman.

We had no ears which angered them.
They called us root-diggers.
We called them hard shoes.
When Chief Joseph rode against them,
I carried the clothman's gun and rode
my father's fastest horse.

Now I carry greasewood and an ax
made of hard steel.
If you are in need of kindling, sing this song:
"Cut some stovewood,
cut it the length of your forearm."
My song is, "Give me a quarter."
You sing, "Make a fire, boil the water,
cook the meat, wash the dishes.
I will give you a quarter if you
come again tomorrow."

Once I was bringing wood to a clothman,
it was late, a terrible noise
came from the sage beside the door.
Quick, he said, a cougar is eating my sheep.
I did nothing.
A wise being does not annoy the *hyas puss*
after dark while he is eating.
The clothman knocked me to the ground.
That was the first time I sang
a blackrobe song:

"By my deeds, you shall know me."

DUTCH JAKE'S
HELL-TIME CALENDAR, 1887-89

March—Began keeping diary.

With mule and dog, forded the Okanogan
looking for agricultural pursuits.
Met Sar-sept-a-kin and several Nespelem
who offered nine horses for a bottle of whiskey
before concluding their entreaties were in vain.
Eyed my father's gold watch brought
from Frankfurt-on-Main.

Near Broken Spoke Ranch met a Tacoma man,
claimed to have sold a share in the Tough Nut Mine
at Ruby City for $11,000!

Today bothered by boils: face, neck, and elsewhere.

May 30—Made camp. Mosquitoes so thick
they could be taken from the air by handfuls.
Broke camp about midnight to escape.
Climbed the hills toward Salmon City,
spread my blankets only to find
an army of rattlers. Evacuated
after killing fifty reptiles. Moved on
a few miles to Soda Creek,
slept peacefully in rye grass as tall
as the mule's shoulder. Dreamt of cutting
fifteen tons with a scythe.

In the morning grouse so thick
they could be killed with a stone.
Deer plentiful and did not stir
at the sound of my gun. Crickets
kept me awake the following night.
An abundance of yellow jackets.
Boils more painful, but draining.

June 6—Pitched a tent, tilled two acres
for truck. Difficulty in getting seeds.

13

Trading post proprietor's wife
at Wild Goose Condon's Ferry
suggested hot compresses.
Bought onion sets and horseradish root.

Aug. 9—An army of crickets came
from the north, devastating my crop.
Insects so thick they filled the trail ruts,
their shells oozing out of the mule's feet.

September—Arrived Salmon City
en route to silver fields of Ruby.
Settlers few—legal land claims impossible due
to questions of statehood.
Three or four tents. A "sooner" named Moss
had a log establishment.
Built a board shack: improvements, $30.
Sold it for eighty to a Frenchman
who admired my watch. *April*—
Packed the mule and headed for Ruby.

Met Sar-sept-a-kin who recommended
groundhog oil for various purposes,
including balding and boils.
Traded him a bottle of Old Number Seven.

Going over Mineral Hill, the mule kicked a stone
which at first I thought was buzzard quartz
but led to locating the Q.S. Mine.
Kept a sharp lookout for rattlers,
particularly the black variety.
A timber serpent will coil and sound
an alarm, but black snakes spring without warning.

May—Returned to newly elected county seat,
Salmon City, made claim on the *Quantum Sufficit*.
Sar-sept-a-kin, who was there with a quantity
of corn, waited for me to supervise
sale and collection of money.

Boils improving. Bought my shed back for $25.
Planted truck in the yard from seeds
Sar-sept-a-kin gave in exchange for whiskey.
Buried Father's watch in a baking powder tin,
north end, second row of beets.

Weather: sultry. Mid-forenoon, a light earthquake.
Remarked to the mule and dog at the time:
"Thundering? The sky's cloudless."
Windows rattled and shook. Later
men in the shafts said they neither felt
nor heard it. Will sell truck to grubstake the Q.S.
Meanwhile staked another prospect,
named Deception on account of it
showing no mineral.

October—Mercury dropped, so cold the ink froze
as I made this entry, despite a hot fire.
Dog shivering. All blankets and extra clothing
used to cover truck. Boils completely gone.

January 1—Today an eclipse of the sun
occurred from twelve until three.
Dog howled, mule off his feed.

A report came into Moss's Saloon:
Washington soon admitted to the Union.

July—Left the dog and gold watch
(with prized chain and horse emblem)
with the saloonkeep, Mr. Moss—Ruby too wild
for safety. Sar-sept-a-kin offered
(for a bottle) to keep an eye on the proprietor.

Mule packed with squash and red cabbage.
Followed prospector's trail, tracing
ore veins and pay ledges. On the outskirts
soon learned that Ruby people did not
patronize Salmon Cityites due to

15

the county seat question which brought
white heat from their mouths.
Gave the vegetables away. To develop Q.S.,
watch will have to be sold.

Returned home directly.
Learned Moss had been killed by
skull fracture, his saloon set fire over him.
An Indian was suspect and chased
as far as Wild Goose Condon's ferry where
the Frenchman pulled him from his horse
by the hair and he drowned due to intoxication.
Moss's body found, but the mystery
of the gold watch could not be explained
—though the dog fled unharmed.

Boils returning: face, neck, and elsewhere.

HOW DO YOU KNOW
YOUR SIN AND MISERY?

Mission at Door Knob Rock, 1883

You could smell them before
you saw them.
When they came to your house
they never knocked and when they left,
your rooms would need
a good airing.

Husband hung two paintings
on the wall, Heaven and Hell
—one on either side of the fireplace.
He took the bucks outside
(most wore only a blanket),
teaching them to plant in rows.
That way they wouldn't have to wander.

To the squaws
I demonstrated bathing, washing dishes,
pointing to the picture of Heaven.
I gestured to their bark skirts, to the old woman
who'd covered herself in mud for warmth,
then pointed to Hell. I taught them thus.
One of the younger girls—the chief's daughter—
was beautiful, she had a number 2 foot
and a size 5 glove.
They giggled. They mimicked me.
They were meek and honest and I
could not hold the agonizing death
of Narcissa Whitman against them.

For a treat I played my melodeon.
The bucks would come from the garden
listening respectfully outside my window.
Mother gave me the little organ
when I married, but Husband refused

to lay his hat on it, unsure
music belongs in a house of the Lord.

Indian women had a terror of hot water
and washed in the lake or a puddle.
I never could break them of this,
though once they accepted my trust
they always kept it.
I never lost anything to a squaw.

When Husband was away
some of the bucks galloped their cayuses
around and around the house,
whooping threats in Chinook
and beating on the walls with sticks.
My husband called it innocent amusement.
Alone inside, I did not name it such.

I taught them to keep a Christian house
—that you cannot bind papooses in cradleboards
for days on end, at least use wool batting
instead of packing them in moss. And please,
shade their eyes from the sun.
A squaw would dismount her horse,
leaving babe and board strapped
to the saddle, no bonnet, no bumbershoot,
squinting into the day.

Soon the bark roofs of sweat lodges
began to disappear.
The squaws learned to make shoes by sewing
with a boar's-hair needle.
It took two days to make each pair
and I'll say one thing, those shoes *wore*.
As we worked I led the catechism, then
we fell to chatting. I told them
what my mother always told me:
"Every woman needs a black silk dress,
every man, a high silk hat."

Of course I learned to speak their language,
though I had to have an Indian tell me
what I'd said. Most understood English
if I had something they wanted
or a child was delirious
and there was fear of the pox.
When they asked a question in their jargon,
I said, "I don't know," prodding them
to speak His language.
They often retorted in the most
emphatic and purest English,
both men and squaws in
a harmony never heard in catechism:
"You lie," sharp-tongued
as the flames of Hell.
To deflect their wrath, I pretended
they had something I wanted,
pleaded for it in Chinook
to the cadence of Narcissa's last instructions
as she pulled the tomahawk
from her husband's head, packed cinders
against his wound, then fell:

Pray God, tell mother we died at our post.

Note: Narcissa Whitman (1808–1847), a missionary, was one of the
first white women in the Northwest. Her husband was Dr. Marcus
Whitman.

TRAVELING SCHOOL MISTRESS

Virginia Grainger,
District of Icicle, 1893

I can still hear it, the tap-tap of my chalk
across the slate. Children, a lesson:
A hundred a year, a horse, plus ten
cents a mile one-way. I led the horse
over Cliff Trail, carried the baby.
On one side a thousand-foot drop,
mud slides on the other.
I'm not sure that mare was broke—she spooked
at the ghost of every dead prospector.

Courthouse, schoolhouse, social hall,
just a log room, 20 desks, 62 students.
The youngest sat on the books.
Monday mornings the older boys were asleep
in the yard after finding half-empty
intoxicants left in the cloakroom.

Before he was crippled by mule kick,
my husband ferried the mail stage
across the river during high water.
At harvest he drove a hay rake,
45 a month, though paydays were scarce.
In the end all he got was board and a pair
of four-pound woolen blankets.

The sheriff—I taught his son so I know
it's gospel—got a thousand a year,
a fast and well-broke cayuse, not to mention
mileage *both* ways after being elected
to clear out those gangs plaguing the stockmen.

The stone in his path was Pokamiakin—Wild
Coyote—a bad Indian with a knife, both whites
and natives gave him wide berth with his

21

Puck-puck-mika, I fight you, I fight you,
though he was always well disposed toward me
on account of my husband who ferried him free
and my hair's carrot color.
One morning he, Loop Loop George, and
Hole-in-the-Day came with their knives
to my door demanding dinner.
Beans, bread, and butter were all I had
and I didn't know the beans were sour which is,
I suppose, what put Loop's bowels in an uproar.
This delighted Pokamiakin,
who forever after favored me.
Hole-in-the-Day was the first native
to marry a white girl, an artist
—at least one of her pictures sold
for eight hundred dollars.

No newspapers then,
I lived by rumor and what children brought me.
Some rode eleven miles, pleasant days only,
otherwise Salmon Creek was too high
for crossing. Squawman Will married
Wild Coyote's sister, raising a pack
of halfbreeds whom I taught,
so I got both sides of the story.
The gangs weren't all red men,
there were no-good whites on stolen horses
selling stolen cattle
to a nefarious butcher whose daughter
was one of the younger ones.
She sat nearest the woodstove, minding my baby.

It was Squawman Will who rode out,
warning of trouble with the Siwash.
Word had it someone twitted Pokamiakin
about the mustache he tried to grow.
He firmly believed no Boston man's bullet
could kill him. He had a mascot
in the form of a bone,
always carrying it for protection.

22

Pokamiakin ambushed the first sheriff
who tried to take him. That night
the children and I were barricaded
in the 4th of July Mine while the stockmen
took refuge at the saloon, firing
on railroad workers who galloped in
to help them. Beneath the acetylene lamp,
my chalk across the slate, tap-tap, tap-tap.
Children, a lesson: Blood is the principal
color of liquor, *cause and effect*,
a familiar picture.

The next sheriff killed the horse
Wild Coyote rode, which was stolen.
The county had to pay for the cayuse
and the sheriff resigned in disgust.
What finally got the red man was a bullet
from the Winchester of a squaw he jilted.
Word went out to our Justice of the Peace
(30 a month and no work on the Sabbath)
who bore him on a stretcher three days
to the mission priest, though Pokamiakin
did not survive his final journey.
This was the spring the Siwash were taken
to a reservation, most pretty angry
over losing their gardens.

A number of miners scoured the county
for the murdering squaw, but
the Indians failed to give assistance.
The docket in the justice's office showed
a single entry: "Dismissed. Death of an Indian."
I remember his, Loop Loop's, and Hole-in-the-Day's
halo muckamuck, no food, no food,
at my door as if it was this morning.

I can still hear it, my chalk across the slate,
tap-tap, tap-tap. Children, a lesson:

The things men do live after them.

SALMON CITY FLOOD,
May 27, 1894

The town built on a piny delta
along a rivulet called Salmon River
suddenly widening from narrow canyons,
flowing southerly,
its source high up the chain
dividing Methow from the Okanogan.

Some said it was heavy rain
and melting snow, some said
it was Chief Moses of the Yakimas avenging
the death of his brother Quil-ten-e-nock.
Others claim it penance for sins
committed before the silver ran out,
transgressions the fire (which took
every building in Old Town except
a root cellar) failed to cleanse.

On Sunday, 9 a.m.,
Wild Goose Bill reined in his cayuse and
glanced over his shoulder at a mountain
of water fifty feet high as it
barreled past the 4th of July Mine.

Hundred-pound rocks borne like feathers,
trees torn up at the roots or snapped off
like pipe stems tossed end over end.
A tornado of water chasing down the channel
gathering debris, damming itself,
breaking with a noise of cannonshot.
Houses fell like cardboard,
the mountainside cleared as if broomswept.
Boulders clicked against each other,
plates in a sink, their grinding
whispered his name: *Quil-ten-e-nock.*

Spurring his cayuse on, Bill galloped
to warn the mayor, but His Honor

had already awoken in a sea of logs.
Later he said the last thing remembered
was being dashed through the upper floor
of Hotel Conconully, not a board of which remains.

Quil-ten-e-nock, Quil-ten-e-nok,
Wild Goose whipped his horse to the trill of it
on below town to the finest farms
and apple orchards in the county.
When the pony mired down,
he ran on foot, his horse knocked
twenty feet in the air by logs.

He got old Mrs. Keefe and her family
as far as the picket gate before she ran back,
"My spectacles, my spectacles."
Only a dozen feet from safety when
the waters of hell caught
and crushed her between two rocks.
Quil-ten-e-nock, the children heard it
as they looked on. Her body found
days later by the instinct of dogs.

Where once there were streets,
sand and gravel ridges travel.
Where there was a sidewalk, a creek channel.
Fifty-foot logs stripped of bark
lay in two-story piles. Even the stone
cellar of the mayor's bank was gone.
The Goose Saloon withstood the blow,
though deformed and a wall crushed in.
The large mirror behind the bar forced
against the ceiling and strange to say,
though the room was jammed with rocks and logs,
the glass remained unbroken.

Quil-ten-e-nock. Those who survived
escaped with only his name
and the clothes on their backs.
Two days after the water crested,
Bill's horse turned up none the worse

for wear. In celebration he donated liquor
which many had to partake of daily
—the smallest dark cloud made them nervous.
For years they depended on floodwood for fuel,
the stovefire's crackle drowning
the wind-noise, *Quil-ten-e-nock*.

THIS NEW LIFE

Abigail Petit, 1890

Sitting on my threshold, I ponder
this new life while waiting for the Indians
to burst into song along with the thud-thunk
of paddles striking the sides
of cottonwood canoes.

A three-month walk here from California.
By the time we crossed the Columbia at Wallula,
the children were shoeless—my son's pants
frayed and short. It would take an expert
to discover the original color of my dress,
so prevailing the patchwork, so ingrained
the particles of dust from the road
and soot from the wrong side of a fire.
Our party was sadly diminished,
some having gone on
to that greater journey beyond.

On the northerly trail, redwood forests so dense
I could scarcely see to read the Bible at noon,
in other places burns gave opening
for daylight. The fires were miles ahead.
As we approached, the air turned dark.
My husband lit the wagon lanterns. The oxen
coughed, their eye-whites reddened.
We had to crawl on the ground
in order to breathe.

At Portland, rain commenced.
Our wagonmaster's invalid mother took cold
from the wetting. After burying her,
we had to go on. Another's youngest soon lay
in a softer bed under the sod.

Descending Mud Mountain, we crossed treacherous
White River five times in one day. Barefoot,

bareheaded, we were in sore straits
for food. "Press on," all men agreed.
Nooning on hardtack
we sounded like pigs cracking corn.
At the last crossing, my husband
unhitched the oxen, swam the team
and floated the wagon. Coming back for me
and the children, he slipped and went under.
The wagonmaster left us to cross a fallen log,
water raging over it, while he conducted a search.
First my son shouldered his sister, then carried
the baby. I couldn't watch. I was frantic.
My turn was next, the white water
made me dizzy. My son took
my hand. My mistake was
looking down. When I fell, branches
tore at my clothes, the water beating me
under. Luckily I was so near the bank,
my boy grasped a branch
with one hand, pulling me up with the other.
Afterward I collapsed. As we entered
a sage valley of shifting sand,
I awoke. The Wagonmaster informed me:
my husband was gone.
The dizziness did not subside.
I saw him at every turn in the trail.

Leaving our party, the children and I
walked here alone. Nights we snugged up
with the oxen for warmth and signal:
a moving steer, a warning
against wolves stalking campsites.
Ours is a rough one-room my husband built
before bringing us up from San Francisco.
On the journey I told myself: as long as I had
a cabin large enough to swing a broom in,
I'd consider us blessed. We carry
our water up from Virginia Bill's ferry.
When we arrived, the river was filled
with fish and Indian canoes, the air full
of plaintive tunes sung in a minor key

accompanied by the beat of paddle
handles struck against sterns.
The women's voices were splendid,
they never tired. Nor did I of listening.

The first winter: a lot of work for a widow
with two children and a ten-year-old boy.
But the Indians were helpful.
For fuel we burned sagebrush and cow-kisses.
We slept in one bed, the quilt so tattered
it failed us. Cloth was fifty cents a yard plus
two days' walk. Virginia Bill's squaw traded me
a blanket of hides sewn with leather laces
in return for watching my sewing machine go.
"Magic," she called it (though I had no cloth
or no thread) and showed me how
to make reed mats stitched together with bark.

Our diet was potatoes without salt,
until a hawk chased a prairie chicken
into the house. My son caught it—our only meat.
I learned to cook camas, my girl chewed
sunflower root like a gum. Come spring,
dandelion soup turned the baby's cheeks pink.

That was a year ago when neighbors
were a day's walk away. Now,
sitting on my threshold, the door open
—I have a door, one of the first in the county,
the hinges are leather—I can see chimney smoke.
A sternwheeler sails twice weekly up river,
alder trees along the bank cut down for fuel.
The Indians have turned surly—one time
some were drunk and I was afraid.
Fishing isn't as plentiful,
the number of dugouts has thinned.
I wait for the valley to fill with voices
and the thud-thunk of paddles.
When it comes, their new song
is weighty and slow, and
the a cappella of women is gone.

FEVER

Anonymous of Spring Coulee, 1889

I put all the woolen blankets, both saddle
and bedding, under him to keep out the damp,
still he bawls like a calf being weaned.
Face hot as a blacksmith's forge,
rose spots on his chest.

Born with TB, which is why
we moved here from the coast.
The only green now
near the river, and even there willows
pearl-gray like the soil.
With each step along the trail
between treeless cone-shaped mountains
a thousand grasshoppers fled my foot.
I walked to the click-click
of their shells against greasewood.

This cabin has a dirt floor and dirt roof
and during the rains—which are mercifully few—
it pours mud inside.
Picking the baby up, I stand
ankle deep, feeling my toes wrinkle.
He strains against me.
Cool him, warm him, what to do?
He goes limp and sleeps, so tired his neck
can't support his head—a newborn again.
My husband's been away for days
rounding up stock.

We'd gone by wagon to Ellensburg
for supplies, fording two rivers.
Flour, sugar, coffee, a hundred pounds of candles.
It was late summer,
still hot, though the Indians huddled in blankets
sweating along the streets. Inside their tents,

women boiled rhubarb leaves, softening water;
outside, open privies burned black by flies.
Dogs and one spotted pig, untended, ate garbage.

We didn't stay but a day, I held the baby close.
On the way back, caught in cloudburst,
I couldn't warm him. He wheezed, his skin
turned the gray tinge of desert willow.
Even the river was gray, lapping
at rim rocks the color of snakeskin.
A bad sign: the happy-faced black-eyed susans
growing along the trail
beaten to the ground by rain.

I've not slept in three days. He's not
getting better, though he's stopped getting worse.
I've dosed him with peppermint oil.
Camphorated water boils on the stove.
I'm afraid to take my eyes from him
to cut more kindling even if
there were some that was dry.
The flies have taken refuge inside. Their death
throes make my head ache.

He's stopped flailing little fists.
Raising his head, he turns his
blue eyes toward me, wiser, becalmed.
He'll live. (But will he be crippled?)
Less than two years ago, I never imagined
such frets: not one egg for a white
to set my hair for my wedding day.
And my freckles, dousing them
in water horseshoes had cooled in
didn't pale them a bit—I cried all night.

Outside, a neighbor fearing contagion has left
a gift of hominy by the fence. The sage-colored
clouds part, steam rises from the ground.
As my son's soft bones breathe on the bed,
a fly crosses his forehead to drink from one eye.

MARY MALOTT COUNTS HER BLESSINGS SEVENTEEN TIMES

Okanogan Valley, 1895

Didn't have but half my teeth,
I couldn't bite down
for shooting pain and who knew when
the traveling dentist would come again.
Last winter when L.C. writhed
from toothache, a blacksmith's poker
burning the gum brought relief.
The dentist searched his bag for chloroform.
I clutched the arms of our only chair.
"Open wide and count your blessings," he said.

An apron around my neck, my chin
swaddled, I stared out the window,
up the watery backbone the river made
between red clay and shale mountains,
remembering when I first came to this valley:
a morning so dry and clear it lifted
the weariness of 35 winters from my bones.
At noon, a copper-headed sun glared down,
sand blinded us. Pine trees on the canyon wall,
sentries to guard my children playing
bare to the waist, even Ida.

Come evening, we lost our eldest.
Drowned. (Tears run down my cheeks now
for him.) Let me not see the death of my child.
Let me not . . . Where is it written
all prayers are answered?
I came to thank God for this free land,
even for the river cutting into a desert
of sage and snakes and the life of my son.
I could not believe how bounty
sprang from sand.

Out the window now, I study
my young orchard, pale blooms drinking
from a trench the boys dug. A tree each:
for the one white woman up river,
a school mistress, and if you headed west
along Salmon Creek to the silver mines, Little Ella.
Over the mountain, an Irish laundress.
Myself, my daughter; five little apple trees.

That first summer, our ox perished.
The children and I took its place, pulling logs
for barn beams. Even as the harness cut
into my shoulder I counted my blessings.
For storebought calico I made our clothes from.
My mother, God rest her, chained to a loom
she'd never own, the drone of spinning wheels,
the mournful music of my childhood.
For the river Jordan-Okanogan and
the garden of Eden it brought to us—
during the first summer not a tree or even
a rock for shade. For the cattail bog
where L.C. dug a pond. For migrating white
swans passing over water so pure
it mirrored the black shine on their feet.

I counted blessings like pearl
potatoes, some gone unnoticed at the bottom
of my basket. For endless sage
—rubbing my arms with it each morning,
no gnat or mosquito molests me.
For its constant fuel to cook game
—my mouth waters blood for each bite,
not for the loss of a tooth.
For an indigo sky undefiled by endless
mill soot and fat renderer's stacks.
For all that has lifted up
my lead-heavy bones, I offer each
of my seventeen teeth

without anesthetic.

THE LAUNDRESS BY THE LAKE

Ruby, Squaw Creek Mining District, 1892

Dorwin, the saloonkeep, brought me the news,
asking: could they use my tent for the service?
His establishment had suffered
a shootfest and was unfit for a funeral.
I wasn't the least surprised,
in fact relieved. I thought it was word
of an accident in the shaft.
Dorwin said he'd sent to Wallula for a preacher
as it was a special occasion.

Husband, a sensible man when sober,
until he came down with Western Fever
and bought by mail a trading post.
There's no describing this place:
3 days' journey by riverboat, 2 walking
Loop Loop Canyon trail with a tree
tied to the back of our wagon
for a brake, only to be swallowed by mire
at the bottom. Ruby City known as Mudtown.
No water, no lights except tallow dip
barely making darkness visible;
8 saloons, Little Ella's Dance Hall, a livery,
bank, blacksmith, and an assayer who's better
at sampling spirits than ore.
Living quarters: mainly tents,
log cabins for those who've struck a vein.
Plank sidewalks traverse the side
of a mountain plagued by snowslide.

The water? 20 cents a bucket hauled
by Chinaman. Turns my laundry drab
and is not without metallic fragrance, though
most in Ruby never tasted it.
Few wells dug, on account of lot jumping.
So far five have been charged with killings

attributed to boundary disputes. All acquitted.
The court? Upstairs in Mr. Dorwin's saloon.
The jury often sequestered to ponder
pressing questions unfathomable anywhere
except at barroom footstools.

Laundry by the Lake my shingle says.
Not really a lake, but the end of a ravine
dividing North Main from South,
though Mayor "Shaky" Pat called it that
when he'd look in on me.
One would have thought his familiarity
with whiskey would have been a bar
to political preferment, but when the votes
were counted, Mr. Dorwin's candidate
had defeated Little Ella's, two to one.

How's the mister? Shaky would ask,
even his florid face consumed by tremens. Well,
the mister recovered from injuries
sustained when hauled up the shaft
in a bucket and a chain link broke.
Fell 50 feet, broke every bone
in his knee. As if the Glory Hole
hadn't already eaten all of our pay.

When we lost the trading post,
Husband went full time to the mines,
I took in miners' laundry. A dollar a load,
mending's extra, not to mention
Little Ella's blouses: high-necked, long-sleeved,
and a sinful amount of silk decoration.
Takes me an hour each, pressing
the tiny scallops with the point of my iron
warmed on the cookstove.

This morning when the Saloonkeep brought
the news, I was ironing Ella's chemise
starched to specifications, recalling
Husband's recuperation: so hungry,

36

I ate starch to keep my stomach from gnawing.
When Dorwin asked for use of my tent
—and though I was truly saddened—
I knew the little rent would help.

"The Honorable 'Shaky' Pat McDonald
has succumbed," he said, head bowed.
"The first in Ruby to die of natural causes."

SNOW BITES

Dutch Jake, 1889

Did you ever meet Cayuse Brown?
Not a miner, still
a man worth knowing.
Did I mention I had a mineral claim
but in order to work it
I was caretaker of the First Thought Mine?
I also ran a line of beaver traps
and climbed the wild sheep trail
to Mazama for the mail tri-weekly.
You know, if you can't get it this week,
try the next. The winter so wet
my clothes mildewed on my back.
My coat fell apart and all I had
was a blanket with a hole cut in it.
One morning when the Chinook Winds
had ceased, I started for the mail.
This was how I met Mr. Brown.
At Lost Creek it began snowing,
forcing me to camp beneath
the bone-rattle of a leafless aspen.
I'd forgotten my face mask and prayed
the sun wouldn't shine.
That night it froze to the depth of one foot.
The next morning the sun came out.
April 1st, two feet of snow. I still had
forty Sawtooth Mountain miles to go,
it was twenty below.
I walked all night to keep warm,
the snow getting deeper.
Every so often I'd take off one boot,
then the other, pounding my feet
warm with a rock.
Was that coyote howl or the asylum
for the feebleminded?
I was sleepy and tired and famished.

I would have lain down, but
swore a cougar was tracking me.
The next day the sun shone with hard brilliance,
I was warm, but went totally blind.
The snow melted a little, making the road
pointed in the middle.
I straddled the trail and kept going
alongside a precipice, listening to the river,
feeling my way over the corner of
each granite rock, around each weeping hemlock,
memorizing their shape like furniture.
Falling again and again, I felt
for a stick and found one—cedar,
by the taste of it, soft on the teeth and sweet.
From time to time I lay down
protecting myself with my blanket.
I dreamed of fire,
the womanly shape of flame.
My only hope was to keep going
the next day and the next.
My ears and nose froze,
only force of habit kept me moving.
I was discouraged, about to quit and die
when I heard a new sound
to the river. Lost Creek was flowing
into the Methow and I knew where I was.
I lay in my snow bed, chewing lichen
to get up my strength. I must have
drifted off, because that's where
Cayuse Brown found me.
He'd just driven a thousand horses to Alberta.
His men couldn't raise me onto a pack mule,
so a sled was built. At his lodge,
the stove made me comfortable,
though my snow bites gave me pain.
As soon as was practical, they took me
sixty miles to the doctor
who amputated the toes of both feet.
Luckily he had chloroform,
I went under driving a six-horse team,

screaming ghee-haas and salty language.
At every turn I asked for a tug
at the bottle. Flailing a coachwhip,
they thought I was coming out of it
before the job was done.
I'd made it to the tablelands.
Winter had turned to summer.
I was picking my way between rocks the size of
haystacks and neck-breaking groundhog holes,
looking for just the right place
—Dry Creek, Salt Creek—
to ditch my mail sack in the sage.

REMEMBERING THE NOISE
FAST WATER MAKES

I was born near the falls
my mother's people called Fast Water
—its noise heard a long distance away.
My father was a white man.
When he married mother,
his family cut him off with one dollar,
never again claiming him as son.

Shadow-top, my grandfather,
could kill a deer with his hands.
He trapped with snares,
reaching for birds with long poles.
When he married my grandmother,
they followed the river, living in teepees.
They did not carry them along,
but strung them in trees. They had few
wants and were never in a hurry.

Every two years my grandparents took their pelts
to the Hudson Bay Company.
That was how my father met my mother.
My mother, who had never seen glass,
tried to walk through an opening in the wall
into a room where my father was teaching.
The next day she almost drowned
while swimming too near the falls
and it was my father who brought her back
to life. From that day on,
she never heard a sound.

About this time a famous general said
of the red man: "Kill them all, nits make lice."
Instead, my father married my mother
whose life he had saved and was never forgiven,
so I never met my white grandmother—
though my mother's mother came to live with us.

I was born in a house made of stovewood,
layers of alkali between layers of kindling.
My earliest memory,
the teepees which surrounded it:
the largest, my grandmother's,
the others, my father's patients'.
In our valley, he was doctor,
dentist, teacher, justice of the peace.

My grandmother clung to Indian custom,
cooking food in baskets. I see her yet:
lifting hot stones with two sticks
and dropping them in. I lay on a reed mat,
fire our only light. For dinner
we ate camas she carried in her belt.

My grandmother taught me:
This is how to weave a grass mat:
make it round to fit a teepee.
Use cattail stalks, small ends together,
and never hurry your weaving.
This is how to make a bed:
bring in pine boughs, cover with bunch grass.
Lay the mats under the bed during the day,
over at night.

She took me to the falls when the salmon ran.
This is how an Indian fishes:
stand on a ledge, spear only the ones
which fall back, they are weak
with no strength to fight.
Spear the strong and you will be pulled
into the noise of Fast Water.
Always keep your wants few,
never take more than you can carry.
One day after my grandmother finished
salting and drying salmon,
she died.

That winter my father left to nurse
a sick Indian. He packed his bedding, food,
and medicine on one horse, riding another
into a storm. He got lost, becoming snowblind.
The pack animal stumbled, fell
and could not rise. The horse
brought him home, but he never
fully regained his sight.
My mother tanned hides to support us.
My father chopped wood.
Cutting himself with an axe, he lost his arm
to mortification. When mother sickened
and died of pneumonia, father followed.
They were buried like the Indian—
only a mound of rocks marking their grave.

I weep now, remembering
the noise Fast Water makes.
I have many wants.
I am always in a hurry.
I have to reach into my pocket
for everything I put in my mouth.

MY BROTHERS WORKED THE RANCH, I GOT THE MAIL ROUTE

Ida Malott, age 16 years, 1892

The morning after I dreamed
of taking a knife
to the mole on my cheek,
Mr. Hanscombe rode down to warn Momma:
the redskins were carrying guns and burning
haystacks—lock your doors!

I'd just had my picture taken
(my blemmish captured for my grandchildren!):
me on the new cayuse with my mail sack
in front of Father's post office.
(Later Momma lent the photo to a man
who came on the stage—a friend
of the Postmaster General—he said I was one
of the first lady mail carriers in the nation!)
I was glad I'd given
my cayuse a tobacco bath
which cured his mange and turned him
from gray to brilliant bay—though tobacco
did nothing for my complexion.
As Mr. Hanscombe rode up, my pony bolted,
then gimped—his sore hoof was worse.
I'd have to drive Bill & Bird and the buckboard
if my little brothers didn't need them.

Twenty-five cents for every letter mailed,
ten for every one received.
I have the Malott to Alma route, sixteen miles
and back along the river. It was my brother
Claude who taught me to drive. He died
—the first bad thing that happened.
The second was the cattle-killing winter.
Luckily Father got the post office,
the boys dug a ditch from Loop Loop Creek,

planting alfalfa, and Mother's kitchen
turned into a stage stop. Now we can pay off
the loan on the stock that perished.

Momma said it was a well-known fact:
Hanscombe made corn whiskey and sold it
to the Okanogans who raced cayuses on the bench
above our house. As our neighbor rode away,
she added: Indian breach in honesty developed
only after a mixture with *certain* whites.
All the same, Momma took us to sleep
in the tall corn for the night.

When I asked to bring Bill & Bird
and the cayuse, she said horses would eat
the crop, founder, defeating our purpose.
Lying on plowed dirt between rows, I wondered
if the they'd be all right. Momma said
she only knew one thing: not a single kernel
of our corn would be sold to William Hanscombe.

My brothers worked the ranch,
I got the mail route. The trail's rough,
—sometimes it floods—but I've only tipped
the buckboard over once on account of Bird
bolting at bear-scent. I skinned both hands
and face. When my mole bled, Father said
there was a bloom on my cheek, ha, ha.
The next day he went away for two weeks
while I minded the mail and worried
he wouldn't come back like Claude.

That night in the corn field, I stared up
through the stalks at a billion-one stars
and dreamed of riding the Northern mail route:
Bill & Bird raising dust as fine
as the powder on Claude's face the day he left.
Up Salmon Creek, encouraging the outside horse
with whip-sting, both Percherons' rumps

in line with the singletree, all the way
to Salmon City in record time.
Throwing down the mail pouch, I tossed
Little Ella a kiss (Father says she weighs
200 pounds at least), on to Ruby where
Momma has forbidden me to go even
when I'm married. Then carefully negotiating
the rocky slopes of Mt. Misery past the mines,
on to Ragtown where there is not now
nor has there ever been
a Justice of the Peace; back to the river,
north towards the border and silver fields
of Nighthawk, on and on to the Hee-Hee Stone,
a rock man standing upright.

At his rock feet piles of offerings
—tobacco, blankets, sometimes a saddle.
The Hee-Hee is where the Okanogans cured
their distemper which Mr. Hanscombe
swears was leprosy, but Momma says
was more likely scurvy. There the Great Spirit
appeared holding a blue lily.
It was camas, they ate it and were cured.
After the cattle-killing winter
we ate camas bulbs ourselves,
though Father says they're not as tasty
as a potato. Momma's potato biscuits
were Claude's favorite.

Claude went to his Final Reward
the first night we camped after
coming into this country.
Father stopped to adjust Bill & Bird's packs,
Momma pitched the tent. Claude said
he would bring back a fish for supper.
Father found him floating face down,
a gash across his brow,
where he'd slipped, falling in.
We took him to Waterville where

there was lumber for a coffin. On the way
Momma powdered his face for his last service,
trying to repair the damage.

My little brothers were tossing in the corn rows
on account of rocks and couldn't sleep.
They told me they needed Bill & Bird
to cut hay the next day, I'd better take the cayuse.
But the cayuse was all played out,
the sore hoof having abcessed.
I wondered where I'd get a poultice
to draw out the poison.
If I could get to the Hee Hee stone and make
an offering, would the Great Spirit listen?
As Indians whooped and galloped
across the bench behind our farm, I spoke
to Momma through the corn stalks,
but she shushed me with, "Go to sleep.
Tomorrow we have to get up early
and scrub the little house out back."

I dreamed of broad pungent leaves,
the horseradish by the privy.
Taking veins from the leaf,
I put it on a hot shovel to soften,
folded the foliage, packed it
into the cayuse's hoof, the remaining
a compress for the mole on my cheek.
Jolted upright awake, the world cheered
Miss Ida's Cure-All,
the hooves of Indian ponies rampaging
down the bench to our corn field,
riders whacking the greeny tips
with their quirts, one slain stalk
falling over me.

LETTER FROM THE MINES

Ruby, Washington
April 10, 1891

Dear Mother,
We finally got us a place and an old cow,
Mrs. Brokenhorn. Land for a place, I should say,
brush so thick a bird couldn't fly through.
It has to be grubbed out,
trees felled, stumps burned.
Progress is slow, but
"Idleness is the root of all evil,"
as you always said.

Most days Willard freights ore
from the First Thought Mine to the riverboat.
I cook for the crew.
So far killed two dozen snakes outside
our door, thirteen rattles the record.
Once skinned and dressed like an eel, the body
is run through with a stake, an end
planted in the ground, the other
leaning towards the fire. The flesh,
delicious, the men assure me.

There was a lynching here a while back and
thirteen reminded me of the thirteen turns
in a hangman's knot and the execution
father took us to see when I was Lucius's age
—letting me sit on his shoulders.
Do you remember?
How one man's neck broke straight away,
he went stiff, his eyes bugged.
The other, father said, suffocated over time.

I've no door, rain comes in, but
there's sweet water from a nearby creek,
a natural alder grove to break

the northeast wind, and a view of silver
river willow below. Above,
the cheerful green of pines while the tang
of sage makes inroads to my lungs.

I still have a bad cough, a stitch in my side.
Would give a great deal to see a physician,
but he's a four-day's ride.
Little Lucius is walking now,
I tire easily keeping him from harm.
While playing in the woodpile he fell,
the ax sliced his hip which I packed
with warm ash. It healed fine, but
yesterday he went to the creek
without permission. Now I rope
him to a tent pole. Today he whimpered,
"Dogs are tied, the horse, Mrs. Brokenhorn,
Lucius is tied. Lucius wants some sugar."
Sugar, *please*, I said.
But he defied me and now will not speak
or eat. When Willard gets home
the cat-o-nine-tails will be applied.

Our home is canvas, the floor grass,
but it's blessed. I couldn't have taken
another night on the Post Office floor
which is a lean-to room in back of the "Inn."
The vermin were the thing.
If I didn't get to sleep before the bed bugs
crawled out of the wall over
my face, I could just as well forget
about slumber, though Willard dozes
through anything.

For the first time in my marriage
I said "Will" and "Won't,"
putting my foot down. Felt unworthy, but
after I began, there was no
going back and now here I am
under my own roof, having everything

my way, grinding hominy in a handmill
for the teamsters' dinner.
One Swede wants to quit, $20 dollars
a month isn't enough. He's always begging
sympathy for his lame leg and stays
three-to-four days on a drunk,
the only cure for rheumatism.
I don't miss him, though Willard complains.

They lynched the Injun killer of Sam Cole,
a man who freighted with Willard.
Willy brought me home a foot-length
of the rope for luck, paid one dollar.
Chips of the hanging limb
went for about the same.

I'll send some sage leaves
with this letter. In your next post
could you write out your recipe for salt
rising bread? I am saving sugar bags
and flour sacks to make little gowns,
else the new baby will have no wardrobe.

Believe I have said all that I have
energy to write. Hope
we'll soon have a hard visit
face to face before we meet
where parting never comes.
Lucius remembers you in his prayers.
God willing, next time I put ink
to paper, I'll have a baby girl
to whom to recite your
good-wife-makes-a good-husband maxim:

What you are to be, you are now becoming,
So hold and thread the needle, daughter,
Work not words is proof of love.

With more affection than I can pen,
Your Eldest, Maudeen.

51

THE FIRST LAW OF HEAVEN

Virginia Hancock Grainger

Haunted? You might say so.
I hear voices, usually mother's
and others' long dead—one, a man
to whom I was never introduced:

As he spoke, his silver star
glistened near his left suspender.
I stood in front of my tent
pitched next to the one-room school.
I'd been waterproofing
sail cloth with axle grease, my hands
the color of his black-angus chaps.
Elocution, spelling, deportment lessons,
all the while mentally writing
Betty had some bitter batter.
He repeated his question,
behind him a snake ribbon of alkali dust
where he'd galloped out from Sodom,
also known as Ruby City.
My reply? (*Betty had no butter,*
my tongue never tripped.)
"I only answer to the Laws of Heaven."

When I was two, my auburn hair
and the red shoes Father bought me
saved my life. But staring down the long shaft
of this "court-appointed" gun
—*bitter batter better*—I knew
only God could save me this time.

Raising my chin, my ancestors
assembled behind me.
On Mother's side, President Arthur,
on Father's, General Lee.
Mother traced my history back to John

Hancock before our branch of the family
migrated to Virginia. "Namesake, Keepsake,"
she sang as I slept beside her,
during her first lying-in.

On their honeymoon, my parents crossed
the Isthmus to visit Puget Sound.
Of course Mother brought Mammy and
a different dotted swiss dress for each day
of the week. Sunday—indigo, Monday—violet.
But the fir island fog was thick and rainbows
could not be seen. Mammy took a chill
and died. The North-South war broke out.
Father sought his fortune at the mines
while Mother taught at the fort.
"Namesake, Keepsake," she sang
as she took me to work, age six weeks.
Pupils often digressed from *Betty, Betty
make your batter better,*
to rock my cradle or bounce me on their knees.

At two, I was kidnapped by Neah Indians
who murdered Colonel Ebey, his severed head
their trophy. If it weren't for my auburn hair
and scarlet shoes, I'd have suffered the same.
As the culprit stepped into his canoe,
father fired. The Neah dropped me.
After that, we slept at the blockhouse.
My first memory: an Indian char woman
bathing in salal, trying to dye her skin
the scarlet of my shoes.

But the Winchester leveled at my heart now
wasn't held by any savage.
Though I always wore a touch of red for luck,
Judge Hanke's cleft-chinned messenger
hadn't a craving for the color.
There was the click of hammer-cock
like a door locking.
What ran through my mind?

Lessons, lessons, *batter, batter, Betty's bitters*
and Mother's words: "Virginia,
Order is the First Law of Heaven;
Preparedness, the Second."

At eighteen I attended the Normal.
Mother had me elected first
female superintendent at the fort—I still
have my certificate written in longhand,
dated 1880, the 11th of November. Soon after,
I married a hop farmer, Jimmy Grainger.
When those vines flowered,
I thought I'd sailed to Corinth, but
our baby's asthma threatened to turn tubercular.
We sought dry climate, homesteading
here along the Okanogan.
Ours was a small trading stop,
I was postmistress.
Where they built the main streets of Alma
was our cow pasture.
My patronage? Largely redmen
who were friendly and spoke Chinook
so that I could understand.
Mother wrote her Old Dominion classmates:
all the prominent chiefs used my mail stop
—Moses, Joseph, Aeneas, William Three Mountain.

The events of the cattle-killing winter,
followed by floods and typhoid,
I shall pass over—
we were sick as well as ruined.
By day I took in laundry, at night by lamplight,
wrote letters for Billy Three Mountain
whose Spokane lawyer penned replies.
Though counselor and I exchanged postscripts,
nothing came of it as some implied.

I began teaching.
Again elected superintendent, Mother said
I reigned from the Canadian line

to the Wenatchee River.
Baby Frank and I rode fifty saddle-weary
miles across sage and saltwort creeks
to start a school, teach a month, turning it over
to someone in the district:
Miss Laura Bailey at Spring Coulee;
at Ruby City, Mattie Farley
who married the banker.
Near Haystack Rock, Miss Ida Malott.

But it wasn't one of my girls or any student
who prompted me to quote from history,
Shoot if you must this old gray head—
the author a confederate of my great-great uncle's.
The messenger informed me
I'd been removed from office. He
demanded the books. My tongue tripped
(better, batter, bitters), my hair turning
the iron color of my will.

Of all my districts, it was Sodom's Ruby City
that brought me grief. Thirty students?
Only half attended school—sporadically—
due to a "floating" population.
The "elders" wanted to bond a fancy building,
four "classrooms" downstairs, a city hall above.
My other schools were twelve-by-ten
hand-hewn logs, most built without a nail.
Ruby was a silver mining town
with an opium trade that never slept.
Schoolhouse? I suspected a greater need
for gambling tables and refused to sign the bond,
but work went ahead without me.
Judge Hanke (his court convened above the saloon)
brought up the point that as a woman
I was ineligible for office,
a messenger was sent demanding the books.

My reply?
I promised to stand my ground until God

or the supreme court directed otherwise.
I will not deny my hands trembled
or that furrows deep as wagon ruts
cut across my brow.

The end result?
Every Monday morning my older boys fought
for ivory chips and playing cards
left over from what was politely called a "social."
Months later with the silver standard
abandoned, the town went broke.
I wasn't paid for years and then
only by an Act of Congress.

Some miles away, a brick school was built
which bears my name and Mother's birthplace;
Order is the First Law of Heaven;
Preparedness, the Second
in bold letters above the entry.
The proof of that inscription?
Except for a ghostly pine at a bend in the trail,
within a decade God struck down
every remnant of Ruby City.

HAYING ON THE SIMILKAMEEN

Olive Jane, July 1896

Cooking for a hay crew, I didn't know
which was worse, the teakettle heat
of the house or the sun, bright as a scythe blade,
burning the back of the parchment-
skinned jeweler's son. Wiping sweat pearls
from his brow, he raked meadow grass
awaiting the cart driven by the banker, Mr. Monc.
The whole town shut down to get in the crop.
My first time working out: 6 weeks of up at dawn,
get a good fire, slice potatoes boiled
the night before. Up late last night hauling
water from the Similkameen, I fell asleep
to the chopping of stovewood—my head throbbed
like a toothache to the swing of Little Ella's axe.
The devil's own kitchen, my father said;
still he bade me go. Breakfast cooked
by first light, men to the fields despite the dew.
Among the crew, the sheriff, the butcher,
a man from the mines with posture
like a drill bit. While I fried potatoes, Ella walked

to the ice cave, fetching sausage and ham.
Not an extra hand to churn, we used snow-white
lard on toast heaped with groundcherry jelly.
Heating water for dishes, the teakettle sang
to the coffee cups, the floor, the table
covered with potato parings. More river water
—would Mr. Monc's teller help me but once?
My right arm was almost twice as big
around as my left. Dishes, dishes;
dishes done. Peeling vegetables for dinner,
I killed the feeling in my thumb.
We worked to the *zick, zick* of scythe blades,
putting bread in the oven. Bread out. Pans washed.
In Big Bend country, southeast of here,
Little Ella said they had horse-drawn mowers
and horse-drawn rakes. Teams of twenty!
While in this narrow valley, along a ribbon
narrow river, Alpine haying, she called it
and spit blood into the chamber pot,
kneading two loaves at once.
Ella used to run the Hotel Nighthawk
until the silver ran out. She smoked corn cob
pipes, weighed more than a man—luckily
mosquitoes didn't favor her tobacco
anymore than I. Lucifer's own, my father
would have said. He'd never have let me come,
except for the new law: a beef cow
could no longer be used to pay taxes.
Zick, zick, cash crop, cash
crop, the axe-and-scythe rhythm cutting into
the desert side of the Cascade hills, caught
in scraggy pines blackened by fire.
Dinner over, more wood for the stove, more dishes,
peach cobbler to make—the jeweler's son
asked me for seconds. Potatoes boiled for supper,
for tomorrow's breakfast, potatoes and potato
peelings and dishes and buckets of water.
Sundown, the *zick, zick* turned to night noises
of men on the porch: tobacco chew, bottle knock,
Satan's fiddle, and foot stomp. In the moonlight,
haystacks rose to the heavens like bread.

The aroma of new-mown grass stronger than
the smell of my sweat-stained dress, the ache
in my back, my right arm, the cramp in my foot.
I sat down in a chair hard and upright as a pew,
bathed in hay perfume. Ella put her pipe aside,
quitting the kitchen for the porch. In a minute
I'd get up, throw the dishwater out,
clean the stove, spread the ash (while catching
sight of the jeweler's son's Angel Gabriel face?).
My last task: pare more potatoes—shuffling,
dealing peelings across the table, like the men
with their cards, trying to read the initials
of my future husband's name in the skins.

LIGHTS IN THE FIRMAMENT

Mattie Farley Carr, 1896

As my students study the primers, I try
to read their faces. Paid in potatoes
and flour this month, I made a new apron
from the sacking.

It was Mama and Mrs. Grainger who started
talking schools. You needed five students—
I had brothers, there were the Murray boys
and two others, some had to walk five miles
fearing wild cattle and wandering redskins.
Not even a root cellar vacant,
school was held in Mrs. Murray's bedroom,
then at a bachelor miner's cabin
—he was gone all day and happy
to have his fire tended.
I couldn't complain, other girls I knew
at the Normal taught in tents, one
in a prairie schooner. Mrs. Grainger
first taught in a blockhouse at Port Townsend.

The problem was the half-breeds.
Squawman Wilcox's boy chewed tobacco,
used rough language, and though
the bench had no back,
always lounged in his seat.
School was twelve feet by ten,
with a four-by-six blackboard, an excellent
eraser made of fur and sheepskin.
I had to use carpenter's chalk while Mrs. Grainger
sent all the way to Portland for a crayon.
The seats were benches or cedar boards
fastened to the wall, water carried
from a spring, except in fall when it ran dry
and each scholar brought a bottle.

There were a few homemade desks,
one shelf for books, one low bench with a back
for the smallest children. The chimney
was sticks and clay and never smoked.

It was a short term, three months
(later lengthened to six) during winter only,
except when prohibited by snow which sometimes
drifted so high we had to exit through the window.
School was over when the cattle freshened
—children had to milk and work the ranches.
Some scholars already knew
their ABC's like Mama taught me, others
couldn't hold a crayon.
Three-month session to three-month session,
generally all forgot what they knew.

The Normal, east of here in a railroad town,
required a month of study.
I'd never seen a train, nor an iron trail.
Paths between houses widened into roads,
some paved in brick with not a cloud of dust.
The buildings were made of milled lumber
and painted. Most town ladies owned more
than one dress—some wouldn't leave the house
in flour sacking. My bedfellow and I taught
each other our evening prayers and on Saturdays
washed one another's hair. For the first time
in my life my fingernails were clean.

Wanting to look my best for final inquiry,
I washed my gloves the night before. The fire
went out, in the morning they were wet.
Outside, snow as white as my gloves covered
the ground. On my way to the superintendent's
my fingers went numb. When he asked me to
write a third grade examination, my hand
would not bend around the quill.
He took the pen and wrote it for me.
Then opening the Bible, he commanded: Recite.

From the beginning. When I got to Genisis: l4,
he presented me a certificate.

As I study their faces, the Wilcox boy carves
ABC into his bench, then prods his sister
with a pocket blade. She grunts in protest.
Some scholars have no shoes, their feet
reddened by cold. The youngest Murray boy's
persistent cough is worse, his brother sick
with scarlet fever. I remember:
as the superintendent shook my hand
he repeated after me, *"Let there be lights
in the firmament*—and let that be
a comfort to you, Miss Mattie Farley."

MONDAY: Poppa's Trousers, My Apron, Momma's Handkerchiefs, and a Hymn

Nighthawk, 1892

Before the sun was over Wolf Tooth Mountain,
Momma had her dust hat on, cleaning
out the chimney, her voice high
and strong—*how can I keep from singing?*
—as Poppa went off to the mine.
With the pocket knife he gave me, I'd whittled
kindling the night before,
then got up early, lit it, and was down
at the creek with a wooden bucket.
Four trips—*while to that rock I'm clinging*—
to fill the boiler. My little knife
had a pearl handle and made me feel like
royalty to use it. Momma peeled
sheets from the beds, careful of the kerosene
cans the bedposts stood in—bedbugs died there.
First white clothes, adding a little lye
to break the water. *My life rolls on
in endless song*—skimming off the scum
was my job. Together we rubbed sheets
across the board. I took off part of my thumbnail,
scraped my knuckles—stain does not remove
as easily as skin. Momma said, be thankful
for our plenty—both a wash boiler and a rinse tub.
When the stains did not pale, she stoked the fire.
White sheets boiled, Momma's aprons (both for
good and everyday), my apron—I had but one,
the pillow cases made of flour sacking,
our underwear. *While to that rock
I'm clinging*—we rinsed and wrung the sheets.
It took both of us, each holding an end, then
we put them aside like piles of intestines
on butchering day. Next, darker clothes,
I rubbed away my other thumbnail.
Boiling pants made an awful smell

64

of cow manure and turpentine. But—*how*
can I keep from singing?—as I scrubbed,
Momma cooked starch for the white clothes.
It was early spring, snow on the sagebrush, though
our brows dripped sweat. We wrung everything,
hung it up, some outside on the line, on the fence,
sheets covering our unmentionables.
Others we draped about the cabin, pumping up
the stove—our aprons had to dry by suppertime.
It was my job to bring the ironing in
while damp, pack it in a basket.
Then we took a bucket of laundry water
and a broom, scrubbed the floor, the porch,
the little house out back. Nothing whitens
bare boards like lye water, nothing
—*while to that rock I'm clinging*—
in this world. Washing took all day and we
had to be careful not to mix laundry starch and
stewed potatoes. That night—*oh, how can I
keep on singing?*—we slept with bag balm
on our clenched hands, the red, boiled and
salted color of venison hams.

TUESDAY: The White Doves of Canaan

Nighthawk, 1892

Outside, the sky black as olalla berries,
the rain, a curtain across the granite-strewn
mountain, holey with mine shafts.
I fed the stove. Bark burned hot enough
to heat the irons. Momma dittied:
Noah sent off a white dove . . . ,
but I did not pick up the tune. More chips,
she said. My hands were chapped and
cracked from doing wash.
Between my thumb and forefinger, flakes
like dove dander. While the irons heated,
Momma started some loaves,
what dough remained soothed my fingers.
If I moved my hand wrong, the cracks got longer.
Irons on the hottest place, dough on the coolest
—still warm enough for bread to rise.
Starched clothes were hardest—Poppa's collars
and shirt fronts, my dress, the three aprons.
By noon the irons were sticking, the house
a hundred degrees. For lunch we ate bread
buttered, buttering our burned fingers.
Momma dittied, I dittied.
Back and forth our arms flew across
the kitchen table, ironing even the pillow cases
—Momma said it gave them a satiny sheen.
I've never seen satin, but once, a bow
in a girl's hair. Back and forth,
back and forth: sheets flew like
the white doves of Canaan—my apron,
our little clothes (quickly hidden away).
Mama sang, *Noah sent off a white dove*
and she returned with nothing. I sang,
Noah sent off a white dove and she returned
with an olive branch. We both sang,
Noah sent off a white dove and she returned
no more, no more, no more.

THE NEEDLECRAFT OF SARAH
"THE WIDOW" JONES

Stem stitch, satin stitch, *What ye sow,*
that shall ye reap, chain, crossed, chain.

Some things I remember, some things not.
They called the pineweed trail I lived on
Widow Road. Four of us: Mary Carpenter,
Mrs. Cole, Mrs. Munson. Plus
Jennie Bottomley—her man deserted.
I married at seventeen, came to Sacramento
from Missouri on my honeymoon
riding the second train ever to come west.
We farmed at first—tomatoes and summer squash.
The Irish liveryman had heard
of my father who left before I was three, so
husband took me to see him.
He did not know of my marriage or my trip.
He had a new wife (had he ever divorced
mother?) and was eating pork chops
when I knocked. "Daughter," he embraced me,
"Who is this man?" There was grease
on his mustache, he hadn't shaved in days.
Stem stitch, satin stitch . . . all I felt was shame.

Run down by bad health and debt,
we came north.
Our team and our money gave out
on a rye grass slope below Ruby,
so we staked a claim.
Mr. Jones freighted root vegetables
and staples to the mines until
he lost his strength to shortness of breath.
I treated him with eucalyptus plasters.
He passed over three months before
his eighth was born.

I ran a roadhouse.
Took care of both men and beasts.

Mine were the only young children
for miles, lodgers played with them.
I had a large garden (haul enough water
from the creek and everything in Eden
grows in this ash-gray soil). Our raspberries
were gone before my boys pushed the handcart
to town—bought a cow with the money.
The stage stopped here. Settlers and miners
were pouring in. Once a lone woman drove up
in a wagon, begging for a glass of buttermilk.
Some politicians came while I was tending the cow
who had twins. I hadn't any matched china,
not a single table linen. When they arrived
the stove was cold and one woman terribly chilled.
A governor-to-be chopped kindling,
started the fire. They stayed the night,
I gave up my bed and slept in the corn crib
—he left a fat tip.
I bought more raspberry canes and we
planted the south slope. The bottom fell out
of the silver market, Ruby declined
before our next crop. There was little
excuse for leisure, though late by lamplight
I took up a sampler. My sight was fading,
but needlecraft soothed me:
stem stitch, satin stitch, chain, crossed, chain.

On the treeless bluff south of us
was Hanscombe's place.
You've heard of him. Robbed a bank,
buried it somewhere on his farmstead.
My boys overturned every rock.
A medium was called in. Outsiders came using
magnets. Supposedly 3,000 in gold hidden
in a baking soda tin. The opium was right where
he said it would be near the spring house.
Hanscombe made liquor and sold it
to the Okanogans, so I had no guilt about
disrupting his place. Nights—before he was
arrested—my boys stood guard,

shotguns in hand as intoxicated redskins
whispered outside our door.

Chain, crossed, satin stitch . . .
the gold was never found.

About this time Mrs. Cole was widowed.
Our husbands freighted across the reservation's
rolling sage ocean—a dollar a day.
When Indian Steven met Mr. Cole
alone at Washboard Rock and he refused
to potlatch his load of tobacco,
Steven killed him—so local talk goes.
The body and Stetson found under the wagon,
his skull located later on. (The sheriff matched
the bullet hole in the hat to the hole
in the forehead bone.) Steven was promised
a fair trial which to some of the whites meant
"free on bail." My husband was a Civil War vet,
I mean no disrespect, but after Appomattox
some of the worst element turned to mining
and Indian fighting. Twenty men—not one
of their names ever whispered,
all noise muffled, all evidence erased
by new fallen snow—
took Steven to a pine tree in a ravine
between here and Ruby. They didn't tie
the noose right, he died slowly.
The next day most families moved
into the mines for protection.

Not me. I'd no quarrel with the peaceable.
(Once a buck and his squaw stopped here
asking for food, they had no money.
Her horse had spooked and run off, they'd been
two days looking for it. A year later,
they sent me a dollar wrapped in butcher paper.)
The Okanogans were shaken. War dance,
funeral dance—all the same to a miner.
The sheriff wrote General Curry who sent

guns and ammunition.
The Justice of the Peace paid Steven's mother
forty dollars out of his pocket.

Stem stitch, satin stitch . . . there was no more
trouble, though it haunts me still. That night
I thought the cow was in discomfort.
It started snowing as I said,
I never left my bed.

Don't recall how Mrs. Munson was widowed.
I think her man fell asleep and never woke up.
John Carpenter was in a reduced state
due to the ague when bitten by a snake.
They hadn't been here long, it was raw land,
and the country was wild.
Jennie Bottomley arrived before any of us.
Her man left the fourth winter, taking their horse.
She walked miles nursing the sick
in order to buy a good cow—a sister to mine.
A year later her daughter died.

It was a tougher row we widows hoed,
though all made good, raised and educated
what children God permitted us to keep.
Now I've leisure and could sew all day if
I had my sight. Stem stitch, satin stitch . . .
From time to time I take up a needle
feeling my way across the cloth.
Some things I remember. Some things not.

Sow in tears, reap in joy, chain, crossed, chain.

70

LEAVING IN THE MORNING

Lucinda Ford Davis,
Placer County, California, May 1888

Our wagon backed up to the veranda,
I load the hind end first, shoving the rest forward,
leave off Mistress Butter Churn for now
due to her odd shape—silhouette of
starving child. The first thing
a big crate that just fits
in the wagon bed, inside: bacon, a roll of butter,
cream jug, sugar bowl, soap, covered
by a plank, a hole in each corner,
sticks sharpened at one end
so they poke into the ground—
slip in the legs, we have a nice table.
Husband will sit on it, his long legs
hanging down, and drive the team.
Come supper with cloths spread,
we'll dine as if at home.

Now we put in the old trunk packed
with clothes worn along the way;
in the till, my medicine chest
(laudanum, epsom salts, borax, whiskey,
essence of pitcher plant tea)
and my sewing basket: a half-finished sampler,
a quilt already pieced ready for lining,
and because of my weakened eyes, an extra
Dr. Bright's needle-threader.

Now cleats are fastened to the wagon
bottom keeping things from slipping.
Now clear a vacant place
large enough to set a cherrywood rocker
back against the wagon's side where
I will ride, at my feet a place
for baby Pauline and her toys:
some pretty stones and the boys'

small wood blocks—a toy team of four
horses, and one larger block, the wagon;
a little whip of rawhide strips tied to a stick.
They never tire of playing Going to Okanogan.

Now I rest, sit on the wagon tongue,
studying the stiff canvas cover drawn
down tight to the sideboards
to keep it from sagging.
All winter I worked on those long seams,
the cover high enough for me to stand in.

Now a tall chest packed with dishes,
things we won't need till we get through.
The churn next? Not yet.
Now long sacks, flour and corn meal.
Now groceries, canned tomatoes, soda,
pickles, tins with brightly colored labels
to teach the boys their letters,
the way I learned after my eyes went bad.
As a little girl I could see light, but dark
corners confounded me—I once thought
a freed slave a new kind of shadow.
L is for Lard, S for Sardine, Salt, Soup—
the most popular kitchen letter.
Z was unknown to me until
I smelled burning Zinc at the Blacksmith's,
touched my finger to the word on a burlap sack.
No one would guess by my spelling
or sewing that I have to hold
my work two inches from my face.

Now a wall of smaller satchels
stood on end: dried apples, beans, rice,
green coffee, everything in strong
cotton bags. When a flour poke empties,
I will wash it out for gravy.
Sheep tallow, the biggest tin,
for lamp and soap and gravy.
I was my baby's age when my parents left
Iowa in an argonaut train

and do not remember going without soap
or light except for campfire.
Even the buffalo were too lean for tallow
and no one had time or heart to render out
the trailside carcasses of ox and mule
whose stench screamed, "Move along, move along."

Now, in the corner, the laundry tub filled
with dishes, polished tinware, milk pail,
a skillet to brown the coffee.
We are loaded, except the bed, I level-up
the sacks with extra bedding, two comforters;
the anvil in one corner, a side of shoe leather,
iron pot and iron oven wrapped in flannels.
Now the feather bed neatly folded,
pillows laid on so that if baby and I
get sleepy we have a good place to lie.
The churn! Laid across the mattress
like an extra bedmate?
Daffy-down-dilly, neck thin-as-a-daffodil,
Mistress Butter Churn squeezed in, and
we will be done.

ETHEL & MARY ELLEN
PLAYING BY THE LOG JAM, 1895

I didn't know what to call
that lady in the kitchen,
though father and my first grade teacher
gave me clear instructions.
When he was elected sheriff, we moved
east to Conconully from the next valley over.
My favorite place to play
was in the meadow filled with flood ruin.
I heard father tell that lady
they changed the name to Conconully
from Salmon City hoping to change their luck.
The new name meant "cloudy water,"
they should call Salmon Creek the same.

Though father bade us: help with dishes,
Ethel took me to the log jam where I found
a water-warped chair painted red,
two dishes with matching patterns, and a tea cup
with a broken handle. Ethel said
father collected enough here to furnish our house
which was across the dusty street from jail.
She made me a doll out of clothespins,
a rhubarb leaf for a hat.

My sister was fifteen with a sober face.
That kitchen lady's scullery girl,
she had to get back, but first
built me a wee floodwood lodge.
"Play house," she commanded.
"Tell me what you remember," I pleaded.
Ethel pressed her fingers against her temples,
her gray salmon-skin eyes squinched shut
—the only way to see the past.
"This is the last time," she said:

Texas did not agree with mother's health,
which was never good, so father

and his two partners, wives and children,
came by two-horse team, driving overland.
Just past Umatilla, the wheeler stumbled,
fell and broke his neck.
Four children and no money,
father used mother's sewing machine
—our only valuable other than the plow—
to trade for another horse.
I asked if mother cried.
Ethel didn't remember. She took a sip
of river water from the china cup
avoiding the chipped rim.

At Ellensburg the wives of father's partners
perished from measles. At Malott's place
our wagon had to be abandoned.
Hardly a trail into the upper valley,
more like a scratch through the canyon.
Mrs. Malott lent mother her sidesaddle.
The sewing-machine horse—the same black
as mother's Singer—took careful steps.
There were no other settlers,
even Indians didn't winter there
—ice in the washbasin beginning in August.
Father built a one-room house with a dirt floor
and dirt roof, then planted apples: Red June's
and Yellow Bell—mother's favorites—
one to ripen after another,
enough to winter us through.

The farm wouldn't pay for years,
so father went to work the harvest, buying
a year's provisions on his way back through
the cattle-killing winter.
A blizzard stopped him, he didn't make it home
for Christmas. Ethel remembered
mother decorating the tree with scarlet bags
of sugar, the last in the house. Ethel said,
"On Christmas morning, we ate them."
For a moment her eyes went wild and silver

as salmon water. Ethel crossed her legs
at the ankles, I crossed my legs at the ankles.
This year we both had shoes,
—my teacher, Mrs. Carr, insisted.
Eth-el, Eth-el, the voice in the kitchen
chimed like a bell.

Ethel said: "You were born in the spring
after the ice melted. The first white child,
named for a woman who perished of measles."
Until I was three I thought my name was
Poor Baby. Everyone who took me in their lap
called me that.

Ethel continued: There was flooding,
bloated bodies of cattle everywhere.
She rolled her eyes. I rolled my eyes.
"The smell," she held her nose. I held my nose.
Eth-el, called the bell-voice.
Ethel said: "A neighbor came to nurse mother
who was almost through the jaundice.
She caught a cold, died the next morning.
Father buried her in the orchard
where the apples she never tasted
fell across her grave."

I knew the rest. Ethel was nearly nine
and took over. The neighbor taught her
how not to let a boiling kettle fall,
scalding the younger children.

Eth-el, Eth-el. We rose, each picking up
a piece of floodwood for the cookstove.
"Call her *Mother*," my sister commanded,
running ahead to help carry
prisoners their dinner.
Whenever I heard the word, I thought of Ethel;
but father said his new wife
was a better cook and famous
for her apple candies.

77

IN ANSWER TO THE QUESTION, WHY'D YOU DO IT?

"Chickamin" Joe Hunter, Nighthawk, 1892

The railroad ended at Billings.
I walked the rest of the way, wore out
my only pair of shoes. I'd stopped
cursing by then. It was winter,
the trail empty except for dark blue
sky and sprinklings of stars. At dawn
sun flooded the snow white enough
to blind me. I neared a teepee
upholstered in old wagon covers.
The door-flap opened to
hungry magpies screaming
from a naked willow.
As I passed, there she stood
—a familiar picture.

"Tillicum," she said,
offering herself for ten cents.
Her hair ragged, her voice shallow
as a puddle, she never looked me in the eye,
a Siwash custom. I didn't want her,
I didn't have ten cents. Still,
she followed, carrying a digging stick.
I called her Sparrow Face,
her shoulders wrapped
in an ancient tablecloth engrimed with clay
—an immigrant's shroud?
I didn't want to know.

I heard her weep like lapping water:
At week's beginning, the blizzard broke,
she'd eaten one camas-flour biscuit,
a curl of deer fat. Next day
she found a rockrose root shaped like

a cloud trailing across the hard blue sky.
She drank ice-melt,
ate her last olalla berries.
She'd had no food since and longed to eat
—the word "longed" drawn out
like a breeze caught
in wind-topped pines.
She was maybe thirteen.

The same age as when I left Iowa.
My stepfather knocked
me out of bed each morning:
don't work, don't eat.
My first chore to milk the cow.
Winter, I had no shoes.
I'd make the cow get up,
warmed my soles where she'd been lying
—her bedding steamed with dung.
Next I fed Buck and Ben,
straightening their harness left on
all winter, else it froze.
When I got back,
stepfather held his nose,
grabbed my milk pail,
locking the door against me.
I stole some rags, bound my feet
and left—his name, a curseword.
At the Union post, I got work
carrying water,
had my picture taken
wearing high boots and a warm blue uniform.
The war ended.
The railroad took me to Wyoming.
I got camp jobs that taught me
how to cook.

Opening my pack, I wanted
to do something for her.
She lightly drummed my gold pan.
I gave her the grub kit, trying to explain:

Always speak professionally
of garnish and spice,
put on decent clothes and tidy up when
you enter a kitchen.
You can learn to make pies as well as
any white man if you leave out deer fat.
I demonstrated the coffee pot:
A miner prefers his hot and with few
grounds as you can manage.
Before you serve, ask,
boiled or unboiled?

Her eyes fixed on my
withered yellow apple.
Cracks in her lips glistened.
I could not watch her eat. She sang
and chewed the way a baby sometimes does.

I had one nickel, carried all the way
from Billings. When we got to "Pard" Cumming's
trading post, I gave it to her for a box of apples.
As is the Siwash custom,
she said not good-bye or thank you.

I walked to Nighthawk's many tents
at a bend in a river too angry to ice up.
The sun set early behind rose-hip glaciers.
Darkness ended a trail of gnats, though noises
of blasting powder louder than battle
raged as I made a new pot with a wire handle
from discarded lard pails.
Grinding beans between stones,
I could not shake the thought of
little Sparrow Face.

That was five years past.
Within months I got enough of a stake
to file a claim which, in the excitement of '88,
sold for eighteen-thousand dollars.
By then I'd built a cabin, acquired

kitchen gear, enough shirts to go
three weeks of mining,
enough rope for line to dry them.
On a night so cold I wore all my socks
on both hands and feet and two
wool caps at once, I dreamed of her
ragged hair, hand clutching a tablecloth
to her breast. "I long to eat," howled
through the wall chinks.
Come morning, I bought by mail-order
enough coffee pots for every
Siwash woman in the county.

Some stored dried olallas in theirs,
some kept rockrose root
in the shape of clouds,
a few learned to make miners' coffee.
They called me "Money" Joe.
As was their custom, none said, Thank you.
None asked, Why?

THE LAYING-OUT

of Mayor "Shaky" Pat McDonald
by the Laundress, Ruby City, 1892

His last words:
"Move my bed closer to the stove."
For a moment he'd come back from
the Dakotas, harvesting buffalo bones
to be made into plaster, his bed
six inches from the fire.
Shook himself to death, saloonkeep Dorwin said.
Tremens or a chill?
The doctor, a four-day's ride away.

So cold the night he died the azure sky
sharpened stars to pin pricks.
Dorwin put him out back,
laid across a plank propped up
on feed sacks for lack of lumber.
The alley so filled with privies and whiskey
no wolf would trouble him.

Come white-breathed morning,
streetmud froze brick solid.
Dorwin (his beard pointed as a pitchfork)
bore Shaky to my tent
so stiff I balanced him between
stumps of stovewood without the plank
which was needed for a coffin.

Hands crossed over his sunken chest,
I comforted them with silk violets
from a hat he gave me
in payment for his laundry,
unlike Mr. Dorwin who applied what I was owed
to husband's bar bill.
I sent word to Little Ella's, could she
give a petticoat or purple

flounces to line the casket?
With laundry soap I washed the body,
my hands puffy lobsters, I remembered
his gift of bag balm. Next,
lathered and shaved his cantaloupe rind face,
powdered his ashen cheeks with clay,
shined his hair with lampblack.
Two new pennies held his eyelids closed
—my last week's tip from Little Ella.
A fistful of silver nuggets
(here in this pillowcase, I saved
every tip he gave me) rounded out his cheeks.
His upper plate made of silver money,
missing, though he had it Friday.
When he dropped in, I was knitting socks
(a dollar-fifty each, used as legal tender);
his foot wagged in time to my fingers
working ivory sticks. I wondered
how a man could open-shut his mouth so much
it did not make him weary.

The assayer's black horse drew the wagon,
we followed carrying our chairs.
It was a pick and powder-blasted grave
we lined in budless willow.
The horse harness unhitched,
reins threaded beneath the coffin
lifted down to Ecclesiastes,
to *We shall meet, but we shall miss him,*
and other words concerning
the future of the dead.
Dust to dust—before someone took up a shovel,
I spread straw across the coffin,
to soften that haunting noise.

Tomorrow while I'm boiling water,
rendering fat and ash and lye to soap,
tomorrow while I grate trousers across
board and batten, my tent strung
with lifeless laundry shapes,

there'll be no one to praise the Glory Hole,
no assurances husband will yet make good.
Tomorrow when I carve *P. McD.*
on the wooden head slab,
who will wag his foot in time
as my fingers work the chisel?
Morning sun shining through the canvas roof,
bright, but without warmth.

COMMITTING THE LANDSCAPE
TO MEMORY

Cristal Quintasket (Mourning Dove), Okanogan writer

Age 12, 1900

We gather stones, piling them up.
My sister brings me another fragment split
by gun powder. Inside, a black-orange sunset.
Fire Monster, my father says
in grandmother's tongue, adding this stone
to our pile. How could I have known
I would return to the Okanogan
with such a heavy heart?
Was my offering to Camas Woman
not large enough? My wish too difficult
to grant? Father shakes my arm to stop
my weeping. More stones, he says.

The Indian school was a long way
from the house of my grandmother,
She-Got-Her-Power-from-Water.
I went by stagecoach, heading east
through mining camps and grasshoppers
thick as ash-fine dust raised on the trail.
Near the Canadian border,
our driver stopped at Camas Woman
which white men named the Hee-Hee Stone.
He pilfered offerings made to her—
a saddle blanket, two bottles of whiskey.
A custom since time began
for all troubles to be brought to her,
I laid a small basket at this legless
trunk of stone. My wish:
not to be away for long. I never again
saw her upright.

No one else from my tribe lived
at the sisters' Indian school where
I was not allowed to speak my Salish name.
The ceilings of the brick rooms were too high
and as I lay on my cot in the long hall
with the others, I feared they would fall,
crushing us. I wanted to hear
grandmother's bedtime stories,
"How Mosquito Got His Song," but
chip-chap-tequlk was not allowed.
Each brick sang ridicule and
I could not sleep.

I wore a uniform.
I learned to wash and iron it.
For this I won a prize of a darning egg.
I did not ask what creature would come of it.
On Name Giving Day we were issued
Christian saints if we did not own one.
There were many fights over "Mary."
Teacher asked, was "Cristal" my heathen name?
I told her, no. Since I had been born
in a canoe moving through clear water,
my father thought it fitting.
There was no Saint Cristal,
teacher asked if I would like another.
I blubbered, coo-coo, coo-coo:
It was my white name,
my half-white father had given it to me
and I would carry it. Crybaby,
teacher called me
from that day on.

Reading, writing, sewing, hygiene;
we learned early not to mention sweat lodges.
Teacher gave us the impression
we must be worth our food or be put out.
In this place there were many snow moons
and I despaired
Camas Woman had heard my plea.

We wore shoes, not moccasins.
We polished our shoes with lampblack,
punishment came if we stained our hands.
Sundowns passed, moons and snows went by.
Our work was before us: sums, words to spell.
We had a special house to hide our dung.

In the schoolyard I looked for roots to dig.
Tearing a digging stick from my hand,
teacher struck me with it.
Beyond the fence the ground sparkled
with pieces of flint whispering
words of endearment.
I gathered them to send to grandmother
for arrowheads. Teacher took away
my parcel, asking: What is the meaning of this?
Coo-coo, I cried. This was the day
after I received Father's sad-news letter.
I had my hair done the Indian way,
a hard knot tied with buckskin ribbons.
She grabbed hold pulling it.

One potato, two potato.
Now I gather sharp-edged rocks
in my apron, placing some at the foot
of the pile. My father takes a Camas Woman stone
in his wide hand lined like a dried leaf,
putting it on top, five feet above the ground.
We still bring offerings.
See, here is my darning egg.
After I went away, a prospector bored holes
in Camas Woman's sides,
plugging them with black powder.
I study the rocks in my apron,
looking for gold as he did.
Coo-coo.

My father puts the last stone in place,
my sister dusts her hands of rock shards.
Father recalls this story:

When I was born, my mother's canoe
traversed clear water, overhead
birdsong rang through a rainy dawn.
Because this bird had my voice,
grandmother named me for it.
This is how I became Mourning Dove.
This is why sadness follows me.

At school I made Indian words out of
my ABC's when teacher wasn't looking:
my birth tale, grandmother's mosquito
bedtime story. When Camas Woman
became rocks scattered, I wrote this

Wishing Stone Song.

PHOTOGRAPH OF MY HAT SHOP
AND THE HORSE I USED TO RIDE

Louise Reminisces After the Turn
of the Century

I don't remember Missouri and I never had
chilblains in the throat again, though I will not
swear we were always content. But
there was none of this striving for things
just because someone else had them.
In this photo, can you see
the frills we hunger for today?

It was a picnic for us children, though
our parents had their troubles.
The year before we left, we all came down
with quinsy. We took only clothes and bedding,
a wagon, a tent, a sheet-iron stove.
In April the year I was seven,
my parents, my six brothers and sisters, and I
started across the plains never having
camped a day in our lives.

Mother cried a lot, saying
rain made camp life "disagreeable."
Father worried.
At bivouac I helped mix dough and
we children spent the evening kneading.
Then mother rolled it out,
cut in cracker shapes,
baking them to stone.
Hardtack was our mainstay.

At Independence Rock,
father took a bucket of wagon grease
and marked our names.
Struggling twenty miles a day, I swam creeks,
dug my toes in dust. Crossing the desert,

my brothers filled barrels with alkali
which Mother used when baking.
Climbing the Cascades, we ate huckleberries,
the oxen gave us cream.
Our bodies had a strong odor.
I had no hat or shoes, my braid so tangled
it matted. I'll never forget begging Mother
for a bonnet. We saw few buffalo and some
Indians whom father spoke to in sign.
They were quarrelsome, wanting to trade
cattle for guns. Father bluffed them,
threatening punishment. They didn't like
the idea of hanging. As long as my parents
were in sight, I wasn't afraid of hangings,
Indians, or anything else.

We took up a squatter's claim
near the Okanogan, our first home a dugout.
There was no mail that winter and no money.
The second, built a log house with the bark on,
one log cut short providing windows.
Our next, a two story "mansion."
I began making bonnets out of tea matting,
trimmed with window scrim. Back then
a lady would sooner go out without her blouse.
There was no difficulty with Indians,
I made them hats. My friends and I
sewed dresses for the squaws.
It seemed we never made them
wide enough to straddle a horse
and be covered heel to head
as the mission fathers insisted.

I don't remember Missouri and I never had
chilblains in the throat again, though I will not
swear I was always content.
When this photo of my hat shop
and the horse I used to ride to work was taken,
it hadn't occurred to me to strive
for things I did not need.

MOURNING PICTURE

Mary Jane Bottomley,
near Lake Osoyoos, Washington Territory

We were "squatters."
When father said that word,
the air got wet.
No, you cannot imagine it
—the tiny cabin, mud
falling from the chinks where wind
and sleet blew in. My first memory:
Mother hauling washtub loads of white
snow down the ladder to the loft
my brothers and sister slept in.
Was she praying? She was. And
father would not have her
beseech the Lord out loud
in front of any man, including him.
I wanted her to pick me up, but
if she wasn't carrying tubs of
snow or laundry, she carried
water from the river as did sister.
My brothers' arms were filled
with stovewood. Father? His arms
flailed like sirocco dust devils
on the hottest summer days—
so angry and wild they could blind
you if you didn't lie down flat
on the scorched ground.
Mother always kept my arms covered,
even in August, else mosquitoes'
burn-like welts scalded me—
kept my face covered with a damp rag.
With so many bites even Satan
would not know me, father sang:
nor the plains rattlesnakes, nor the wolves.
My raised arms said, Pick me up, but
there was not an hour when

any of them did not bear a bucket, an ax,
kettle, water dipper, churn handle, soap paddle.
One day father found a black snake
curled at the foot of my cradle. It was not
the smooth cool dog tail
which set me wailing, but father's
long teeth, his rock-a-bye so coyote-like
I beseeched the ceiling and,
when mother took me outside,
the unobscured blue sky. We had so
few candles and so few hours of
daylight in winter. "Many hands
make light work," was Mama's motto,
still there were too few to carry me.
I was a big girl with a doll to care for,
a doll who needed rocking and singing to.
I called St. Patrick to drive the serpents
away for the sake of dolly.
To prove up on our squatter's claim
we needed a house with one glass
window which mother bought with hens
kept safe from wolves by bedding
them under the house, praying (silently)
the rooster wouldn't crow too early, prompting
father to reach for his ax.
Before I was born, mother traded laundry
for a set of eggs and committed the sin
of pride each time she said
she'd kept chickens all her married life.
Fowl under the house, the one
glass window safe under mother
and father's bed while a sheepskin
covered the hole. Mother traded
a lend of that window for coffee
to our neighbors when their place
came up for inspection. I longed
to touch it, but was not allowed and
imagined sucking it like ice
on the washbasin. I don't remember
father leaving, it must have been

the day mother sat and rocked me
even though there was wash to do.
He took the horse but not
the prove-up window. No one
ever found a snake in my blankets again.
That winter I learned the weight
of the water bucket, the weight
of kindling. One foot in front of the other,
back and forth from the river, the wood pile,
until I felt I was sleeping on my feet
the way a horse does. Now you can
see it from the one glass window,
amid sunflowers even more brilliant beneath
heavy dew; frail as the hummingbirds,
two crossed sticks planted where
no one had the strength or heart
to scratch my name:

Daughter, 1885–1894.

AFTERWORD

In January of 1990, I was thinking of a novel I'd been meaning to write about a woman miner in the Northwest in the late 1880's. As I went about my mid-winter chores on my farm in the foothills of the Cascade Mountains near Seattle, I tried to imagine her day-to-day life: washing clothes in glacier runoff, rubbing the soil out with sand, drying her skirts on rocks. Visiting the library stacks at the University of Washington, I had trouble locating material. Women miners—other than the handful who went to Alaska—hadn't left much of a story behind. I recalled visiting an abandoned silver mine near Okanogan, Washington and that's probably why I picked up a particular old book, a compilation of pioneer reminiscences from newspaper articles published in 1924 by the *Okanogan Independent*.

The Okanogan is a narrow, somewhat isolated river valley in the north-central part of this state, fifty miles northwest as the crow flies from the Grand Coulee Dam. Today, in addition to supporting a variety of agricultural pursuits, it is a major apple-growing district. Irrigated pear and cherry orchards are quilted among fields of aquamarine alfalfa. Cattle and sheep graze beneath ponderosa pines on the arid mountains to the west of the Okanogan River, and herds of appaloosa horses roam the sage bluffs of the Colville Indian Reservation to the east. The air is dry without a hint of pollution. Though this state is often characterized by constant rain, the sun shines on an average of 300 days a year in Okanogan County. At the turn of the century, Owen Wister published his classic Western novel, *The Virginian*, based on the lives of the cattlemen of this region. His book spawned the television series of the same name and was the inspiration for the classic movie *Shane*, both of which helped mold modern culture's romantic idea of the American West.

Only a few of the reminiscences collected in *Glimpses of Pioneer Life* were by women and I suspected they were interviewed because their husbands had died. There was mention of silver mines at Ruby City, Loomis (Ragtown), and Nighthawk, but only a vague reference to a woman miner cum dance hall girl named Little Ella who purportedly weighed close to 200 lbs. Reading on, I learned that during their first winter homesteading

97

(1888–89), Viriginia Grainger Herrmann, Mary Malott, and Sarah Jones experienced weather so mild that the soil could be tilled in February. Thigh-high bunch grass grew along the river. Livestock flourished, so more cattle were brought into the valley. Some of the newcomers hadn't had time to build houses and lived in dugouts or tents. The mild climate did not necessitate a barn, animals could winter on the range.

Their second winter (1889–90) seemed to follow the same pattern as the first. Then shortly after New Year's it began snowing. The wind blew for thirteen consecutive days and the snow drifted seven feet deep. When the winds died down, the temperature dropped to 40 below. The only stock that survived were those animals brought into the house. There was no food for man, woman, or beast other than biscuits, seed potatoes, and the frozen carcasses of the dead. When the ice melted, the bloated bodies of cattle were everywhere. There followed an epidemic of typhoid, often complicated by pneumonia. How women with infant children living in dugouts survived I could not imagine. When spring came, the few cattle that remained were so weak they didn't have the energy to graze. The men were often too ill to do chores. More than one woman, sick and enfeebled herself, put her baby on her back, crawled out to a fallen cow and helped raise it with a fence pole each time it fell.

Sarah Jones's husband lost his health entirely and died shortly before his eighth child was born. A month out of childbed, Sarah opened a roadhouse, feeding and bedding freighters and miners along with their horses. If she slept at all it was in the corn crib. Mary Malott opened a stage stop while her husband operated the post office. Their teenage daughter Ida braved cougars, rattlesnakes, and Indians in order to deliver the mail on horseback and was purported to be one of the first female mail carriers in the country.

I forgot about the novel I was going to write. Questions came to mind more quickly than I could jot them down. The Okanogan wasn't always green orchards. When these women arrived it was a desert of shifting sand and sagebrush—often rocks were their only shade in hundred-degree heat. They had few belongings, their most valuable possession a plow. Few owned a sewing machine. There was no civilization other than the Indians, a few miners and trappers, and certainly no doctors or schools. Why had these people come here? Some were young, but many were in mid-life, in bad health, and caring for many children. Why were they starting over?

I became hungry for news of their lives. Searching the Northwest archives, I found the bits and pieces of their existence so fascinating that I temporarily lost sight of my original question. Lucinda Davis and her family, which included four children and a babe-in-arms, killed 300 rattlesnakes outside their tent during the first summer following their arrival. Between chores, Lucinda somehow found time for embroidery. Later I learned from her granddaughter that Mrs. Davis held her sewing two inches from her face, because she had been almost blind since the age of four. Another woman with eight children, a husband, and two hired men to feed, taught her children to read using the labels on baking powder and lard cans because there were no books other than the Bible. The only experienced school teacher, Virginia Herrmann, held her moral ground though she was alone and threatened with a gun by the forces of mining town "justice." The local judge (whose courtroom was above the saloon) wanted her to sign a bond so that he could build a school cum gambling hall with Federal money.

Some of these women's names I never discovered, some I found actual photographs of in the University of Washington archives and elsewhere. Others I found mention of again and again in privately published memoirs. More than one Okanogan pioneer father wrote a book about his life. And more than one Ph.D. dissertation was written on the pioneer fathers and Okanogan Indians of this region. But what about the women? And what about the children of mixed blood, products of Indian women marrying white trappers and miners? Their stories seemed to have fallen through a crack. In 1936 the State of Washington began interviewing elderly persons receiving assistance from the Department of Public Welfare through the Friendly Visiting Program. These were culled, edited, and published in a three-volume collection, *Told by the Pioneers*. Many women like Mary Birsky, who remembered the avalanche that killed her mother, were interviewed and so I learned more of her day-to-day life. But why her parents homesteaded in Rattlesnake Canyon near Lake Chelan in 1887 was still a mystery, so I pressed on. Though the interview (by Nora Guilland) with Sarah Jones was one of those that was unpublished, I managed to get a copy of it from the state archives and so learned a little more about her. Reading between the lines, I began braiding her life into a poem, very much the way she might have braided a rag rug from clothes too tattered to be made over.

I wrote letters and knocked on doors: Could I read your grandmother's letters? Could I read your (very) privately published family history? One pioneer mother was said to have known when a child had diphtheria, because she could smell it. This skill and so many others have been lost to us.

I dug deeper. Though these women's world was far removed from my own, certain similarities began to appear. There was an active opium trade throughout the mining towns of the Northwest, even then drugs were a problem. Cocaine was prescribed for a wide variety of ailments, including conjunctivitis and toothache, and was readily available. Lucinda Davis's recipe for homemade cough syrup called for sweet spirits, alcohol, and laudanum. It would not be unfair to say that narcotics were commonplace. Gangs of cattle and horse thieves plagued the stockmen. More often than not these rustlers were aided by a nefarious butcher masquerading as a good citizen. There was racial unrest as well—between the whites, Indians, and Chinese mining labor. More than one schoolmarm wondered how to cope with the behavior problems of children of mixed blood caught between two cultures and embraced by neither. Drugs, gangs, racial unrest—the similarities with the social ills of today didn't stop there.

Many of these Okanogan pioneer women "worked out," meaning they were employed outside the home. In 1890 it went without saying that because a woman was not the family breadwinner, she was paid half of what a man was paid as a school teacher. When a new district was short on funds, it made sense to hire women—you could get two for the price of one. Sometimes she received no wages at all, only her room and board, the rest paid in flour and potatoes.

But women often did have to work to support themselves and their children and without childcare. In such cases the older siblings usually looked after the younger. However, an Okanogan woman homesteader who was forced to "work out," leaving her children alone, was not looked upon as irresponsible and as an object of scorn (and legal action) as such mothers sometimes are today, but more in the light of someone who, due to circumstances, must work her way through college—with and air of virtue and strength of character. Following the cattle-killing winter, Mrs. Herrmann worked as a school teacher to pay off the debt owed on their livestock that had perished. She took her infant son to a ten-by-twelve foot log schoolhouse (built without a nail) where young "scholars," as students were called, interrupted their lessons to rock his cradle. Virginia herself had experienced the same situation as a child. At the age of six weeks she accompanied her mother who taught at a fort near Seattle after being left destitute by the Civil War. One Okanogan laundress remembered that her mother, who worked as a weaver, had tied her to a loom to keep her from harm. This same laundress was forced to support her children due to her husband's drunkeness. When it came time to pay her, the saloon owner and store keepers applied what her husband owed them to her laundry bill and she was forced to dig camas for food, the preparation of which was taught to her by the only other female within miles, an Indian charwoman. Our social problems and family issues seemed to be a constant, taking on only a slightly different shape over the last hundred years.

Returning to my original question, I again asked myself: Why had these resourceful people come to this rattlesnake-infested desert? What historical and economic tides swept them here?

Their reasons were many and varied. In 1888 a large part of the Colville Reservation was opened up for homesteading. Land was free, the air clean and dry. To those with tuberculosis like Sarah Jones's husband and Virginia Herrmann's infant son, this was a last chance for health. During the 1880's and 90's a serious recession gripped the country, money was scarce and credit unheard of. With the promise of free land, immigrants like Mary and L. C. Malott could sell their farms in Northern California, get out from under their mortgages, and begin again free and clear. Some newcomers like Lucinda Davis were the children of 49ers and had crossed the plains with their parents. Moving on to the promise of greener pastures was in their blood. And where better to set the sails of their land schooners than for a valley of endless bunch grass, promising silver mines and mild winters? Others immigrated from Europe—also in economic difficulty—

101

where they had no hope of ever owning their own farm or even getting anything but a menial job. Still other Okanogan pioneers had been infected with what was called Western Fever, abandoning their work-a-day jobs in eastern cities for free land and the possibility of overnight fortune in the mines. Wives were expected to follow and make do the best they could. Finally, more than a handful of husbands, fathers, and brothers had worked for years building or operating railroads. As the Twentieth Century approached, these giants began to streamline and economize. Many a worker was laid off. Unable to find other employment, they lost their homes and farms. The Okanogan was the answer to hard times and tarnished dreams.

The similarities between life in the United States at the end of the last century and now overwhelmed me. But how, I wondered, could we hope to learn from history, if we know so little of it? Wars and the lives of presidents and generals have been preserved—I had to memorize such to graduate from grammar school. But of social and domestic history I was taught nothing. To uncover the heroic lives of my foremothers on farms a few hundred miles from my own, I had to scour library stacks and private collections and even then interpolate and invent.

On the centennial of the cattle-killing winter in the Okanogan Valley, I vowed to preserve the wisdom and lives of those pioneer mothers.

—Jana Harris
Sultan, Washington

160462